Cozycore
COLORING BOOK

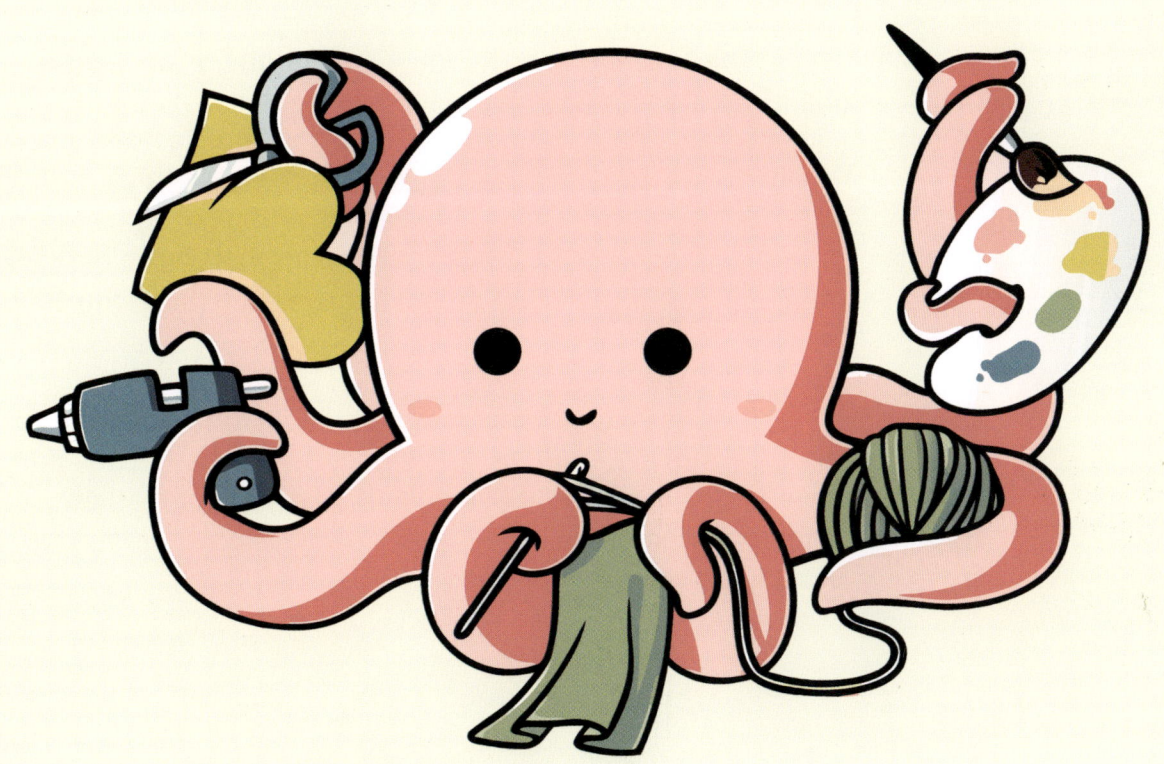

chartwell
books

Snuggle up in a cute and comfy world!

Loveable faces, huggable characters, and hygge hangouts—prepare to embrace the quiet and cozy as you flip through the pages of *Cozycore Coloring Book*. From shared activities with friends to the small, cozy corners of home, let yourself drift into the heartwarming designs on each page as you explore a relaxing and stress-free coloring experience.

Feel the stress of the day melt away as you flip through this collection of cute animals in simple everyday scenes. With no rules on how to color these adorable designs and over 100 pages to choose from, you can explore your creativity in whatever way you wish. Tap into your imagination and breathe life into the cute critters and quiet spaces using your favorite colors or use a selection of random hues as you color in the adorable, meditative patterns found on the back of each page, the choice is yours.

Whether you're a beginner or experienced colorer, anyone is sure to find calm, creative, and inspiring fun in the pages of this sweet and cozy coloring book. Settle in, grab your colors, and take a minute to slow down, relish the calm moments, and appreciate the simple things that make every day just a bit brighter.

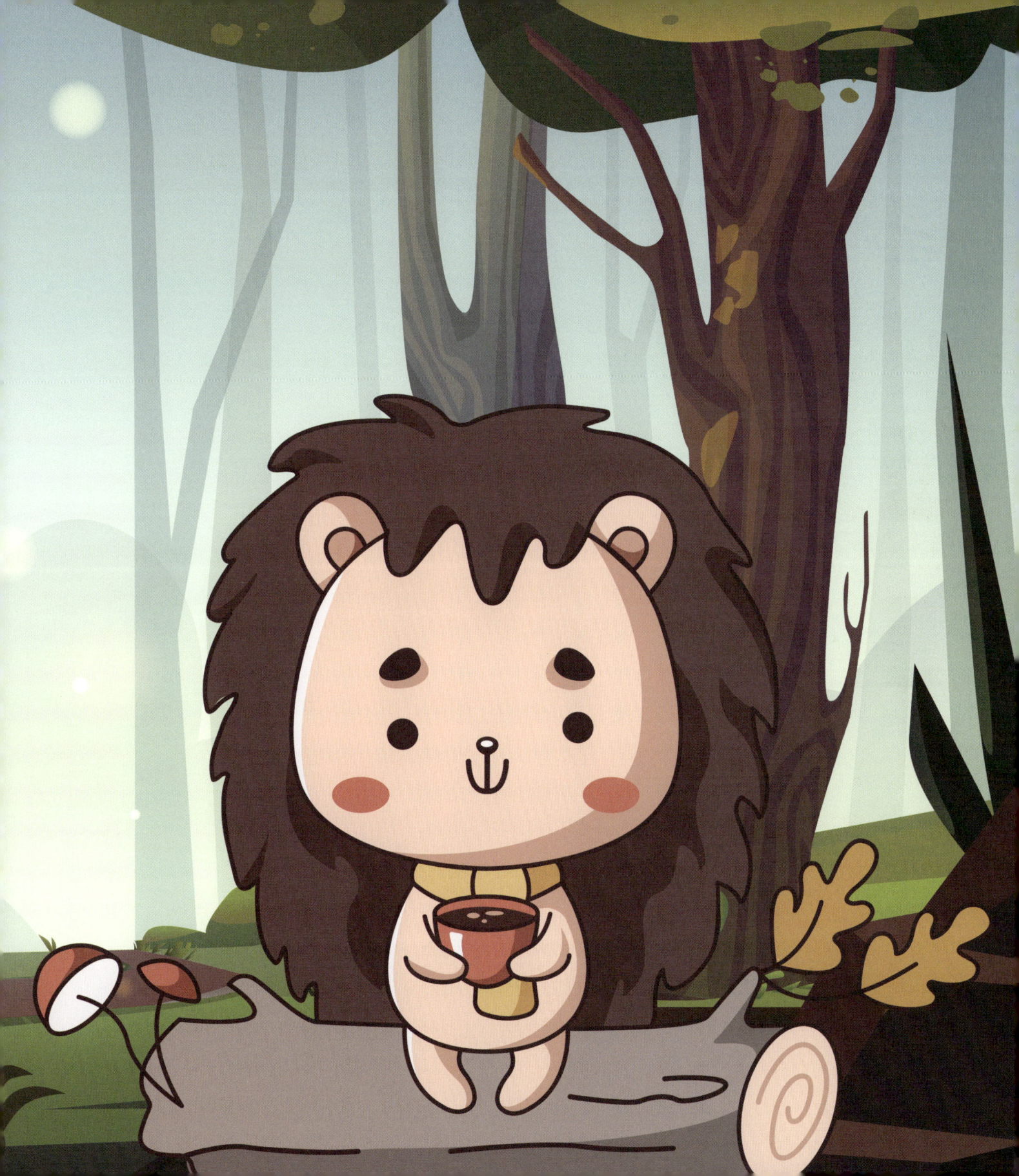

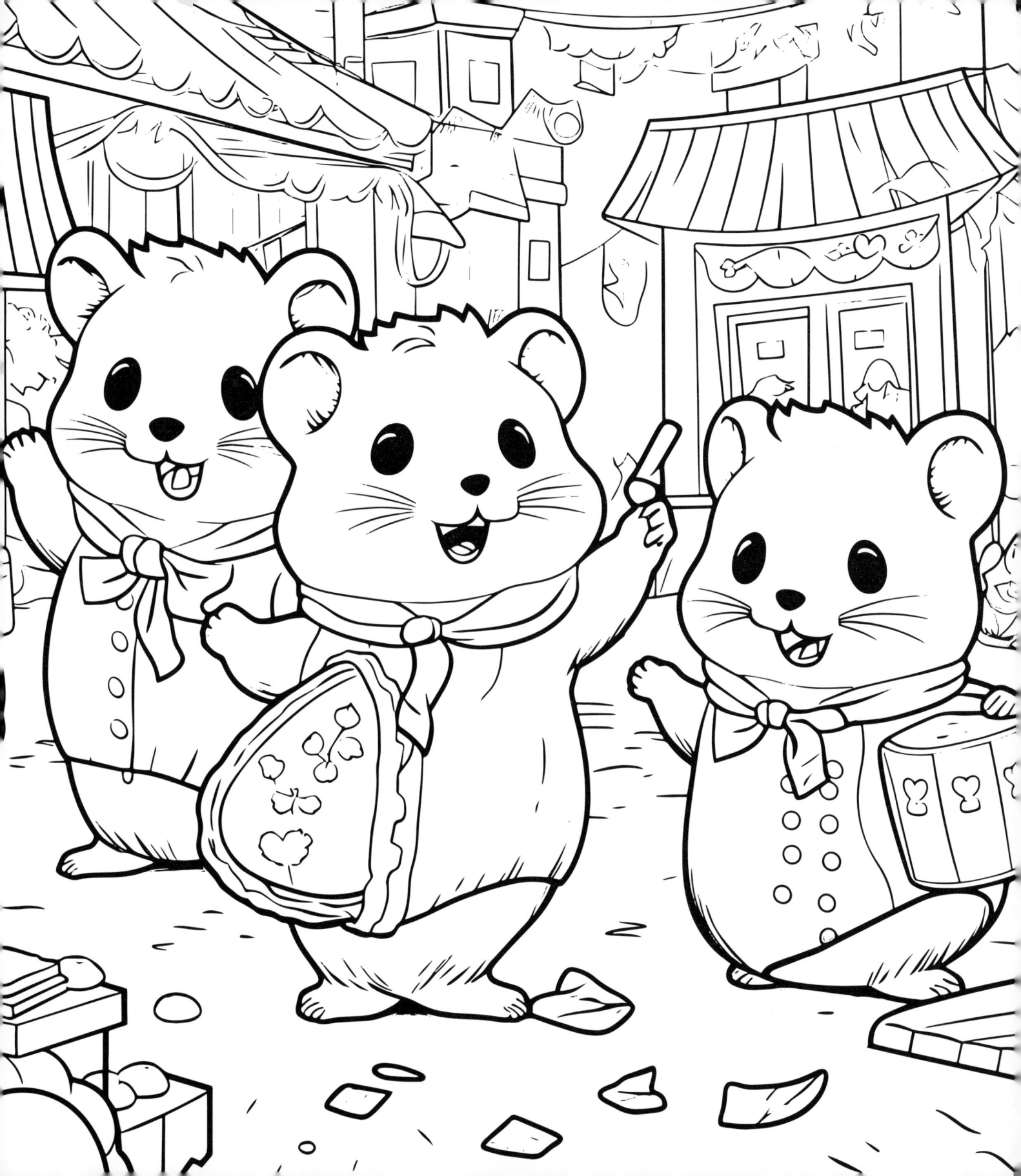

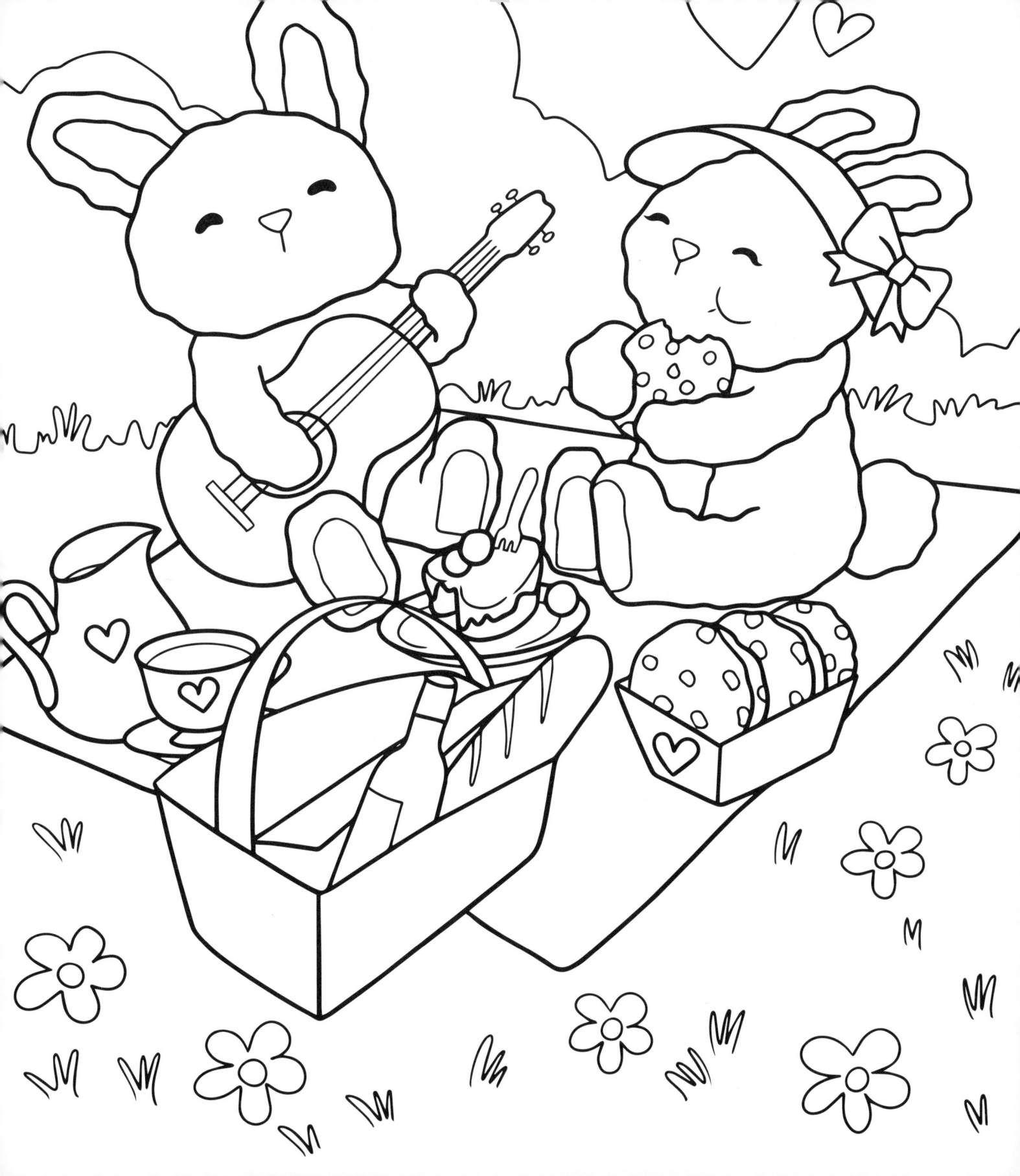

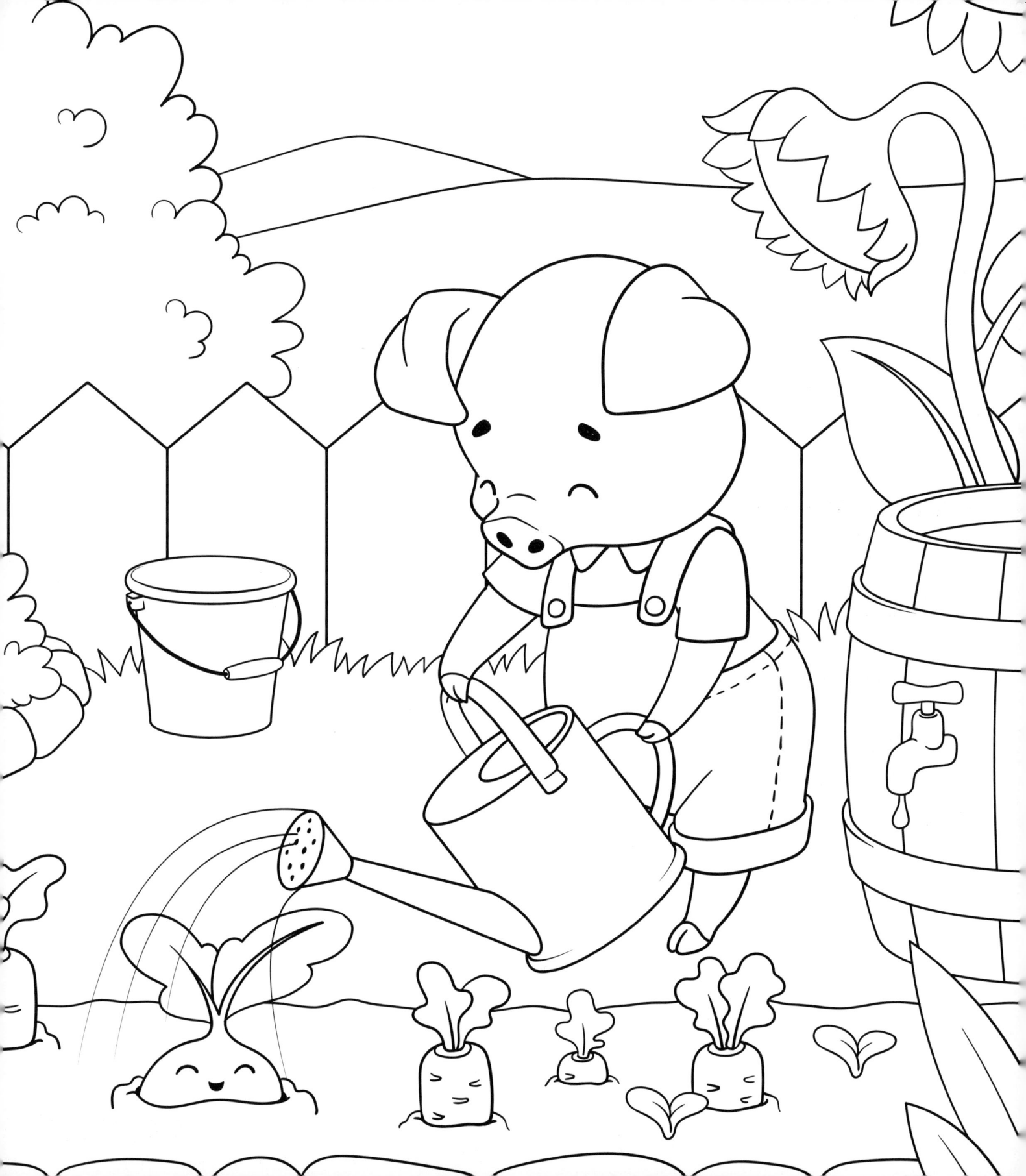

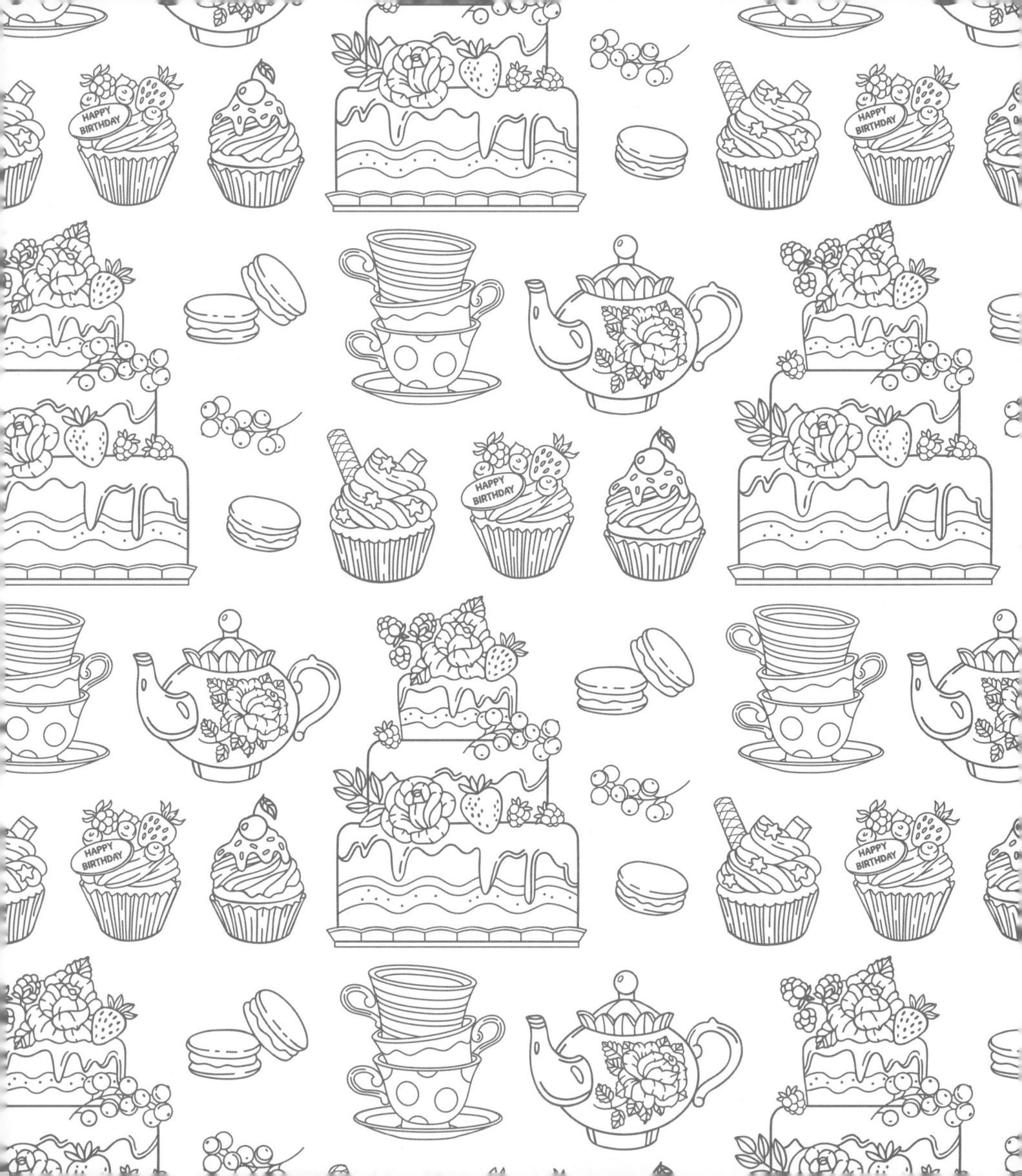

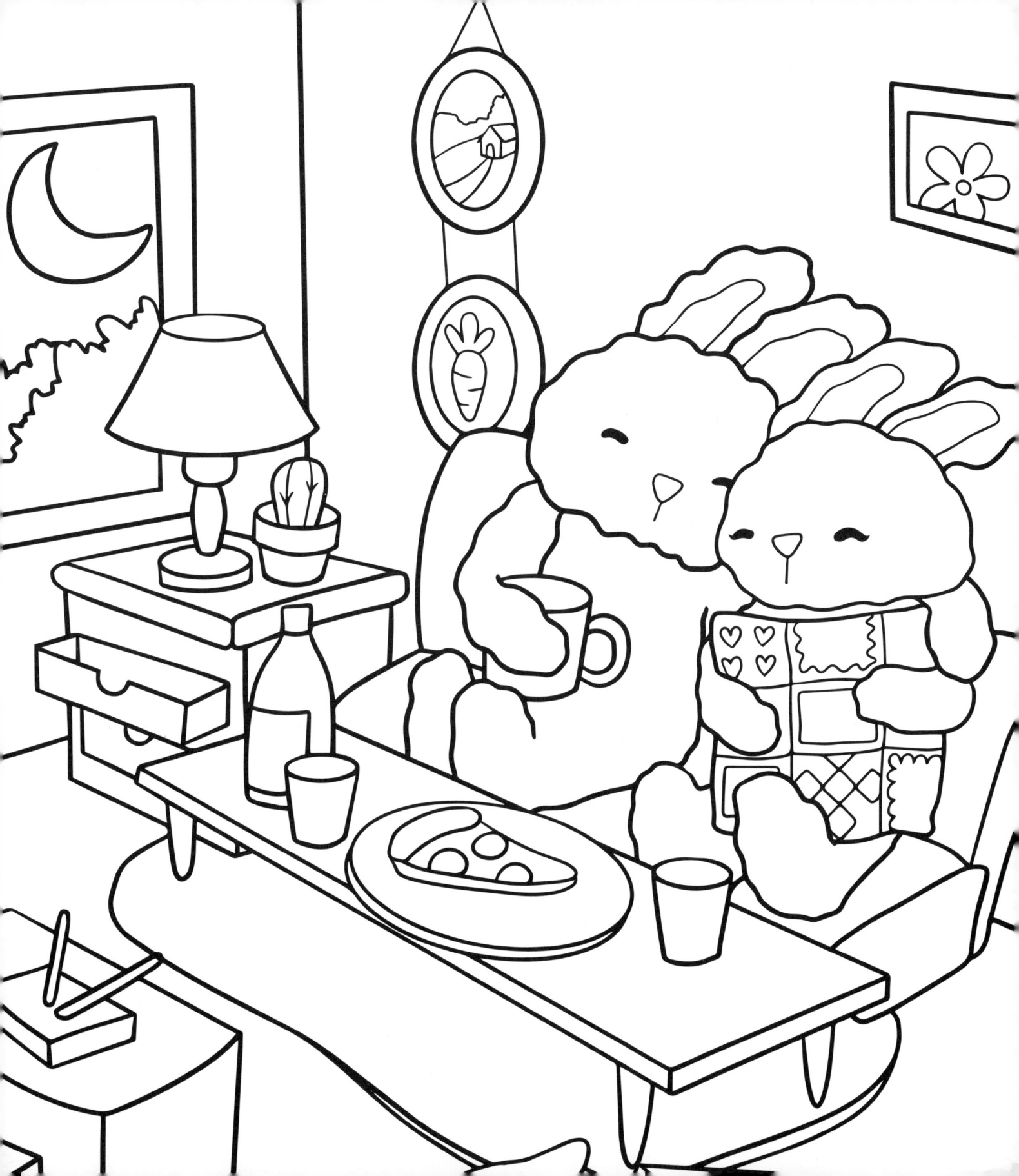

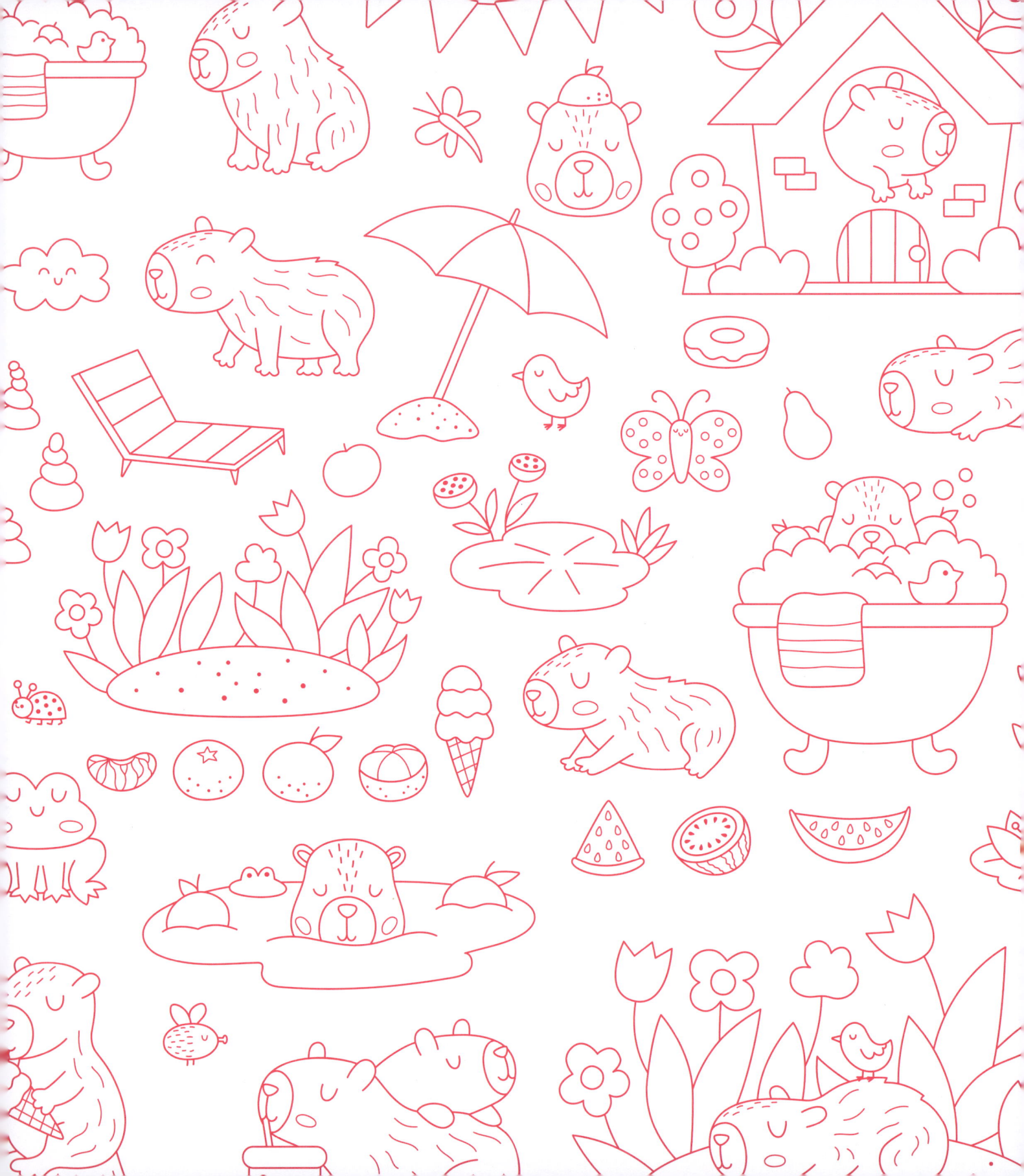

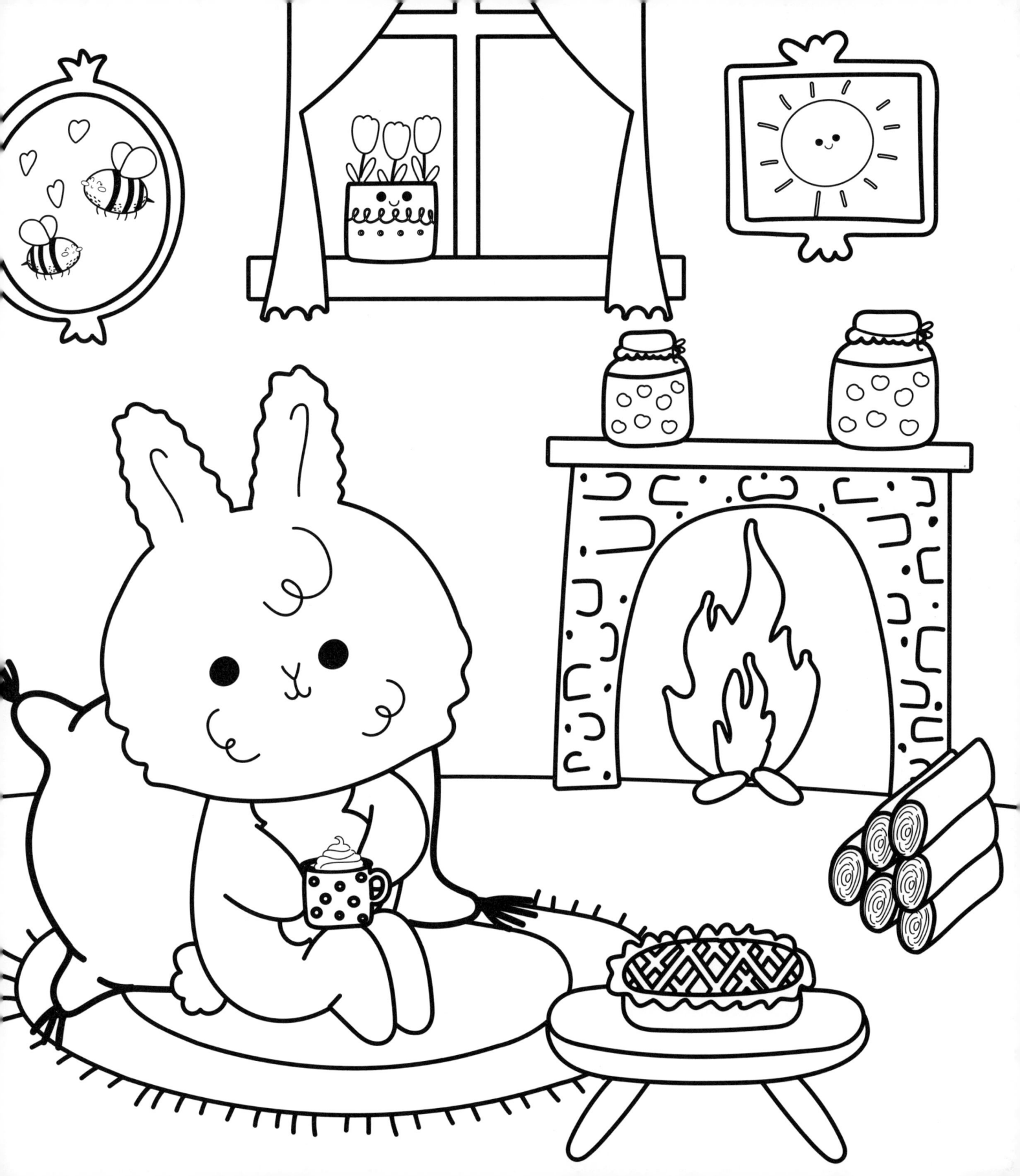

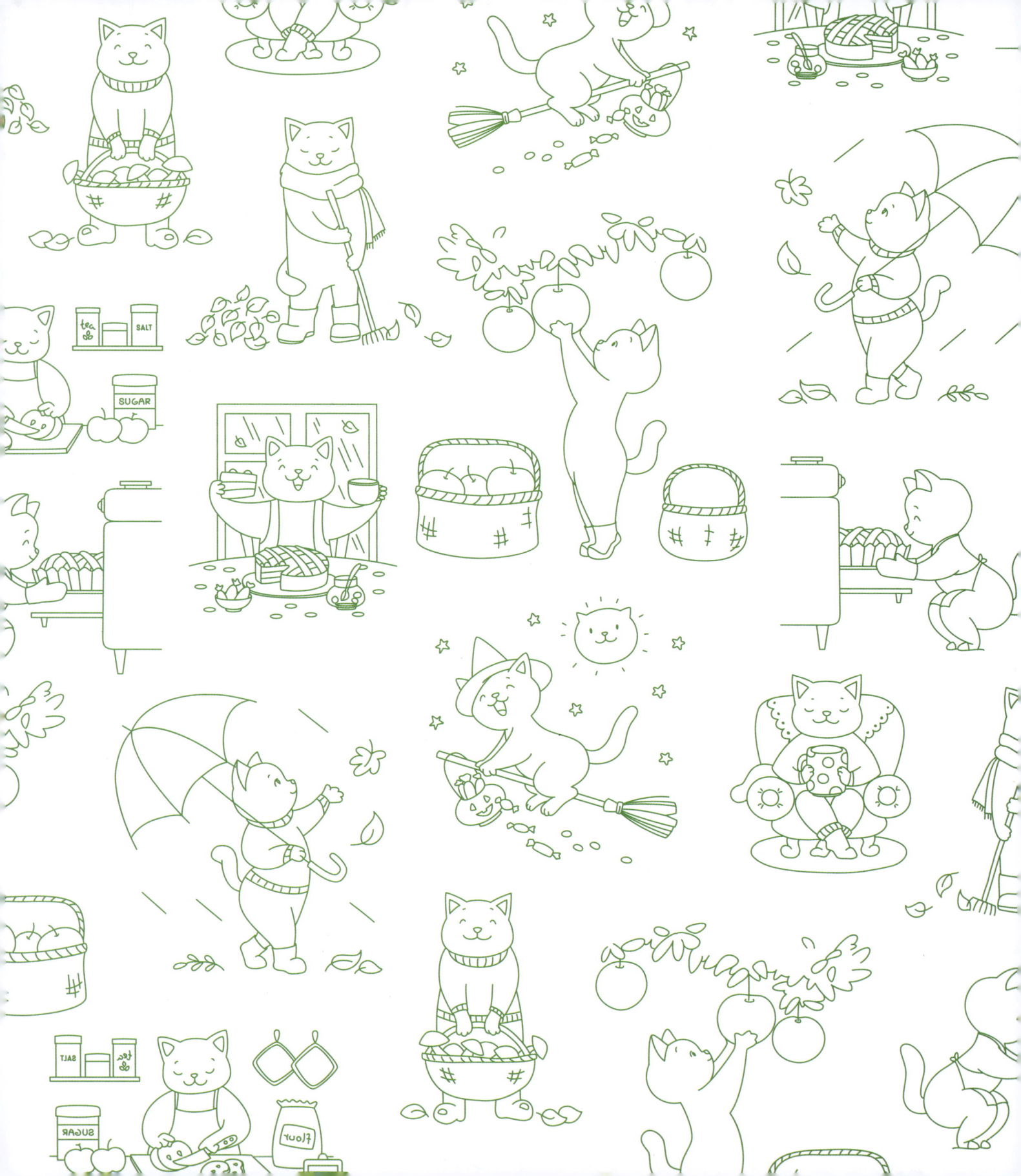

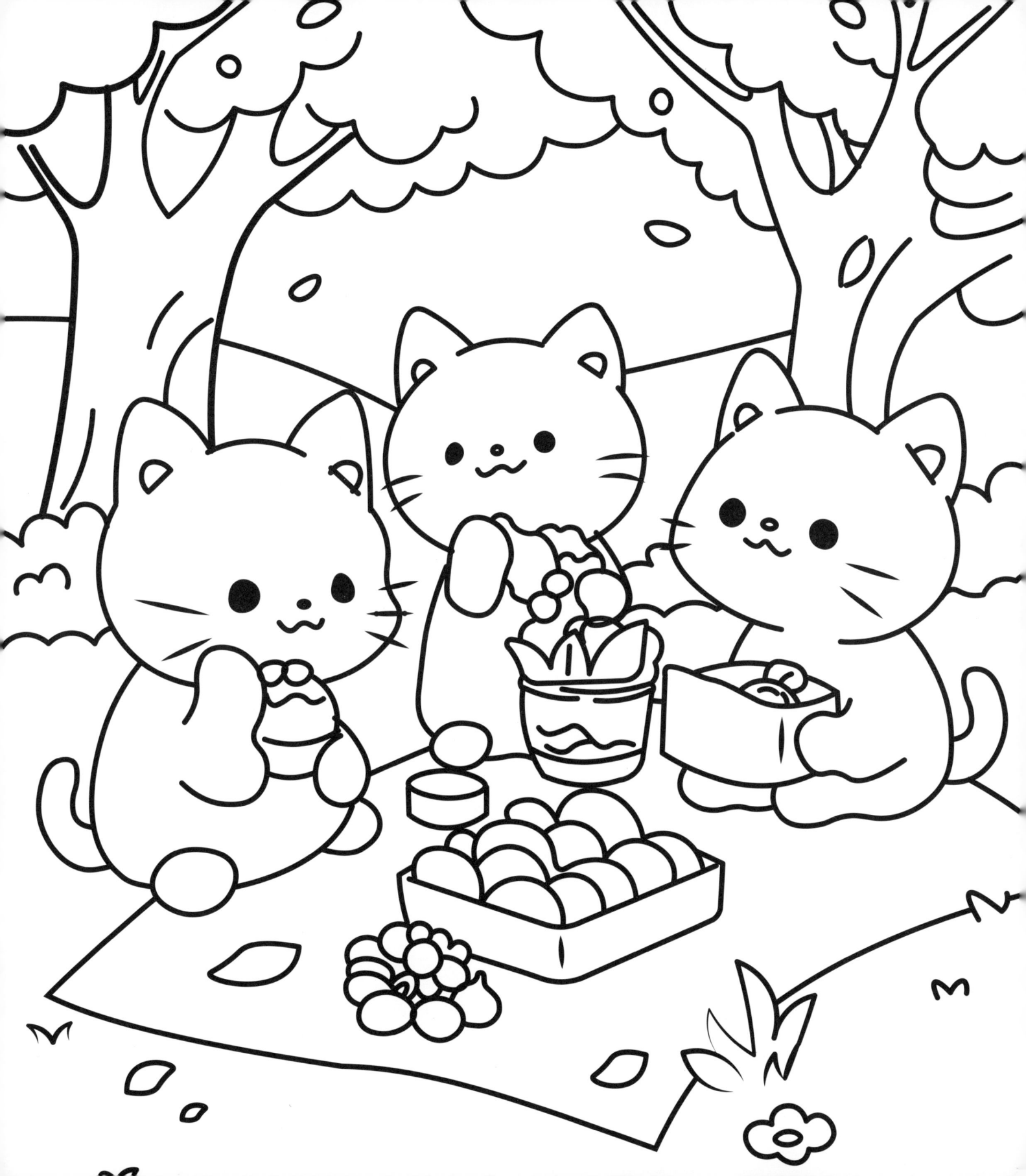

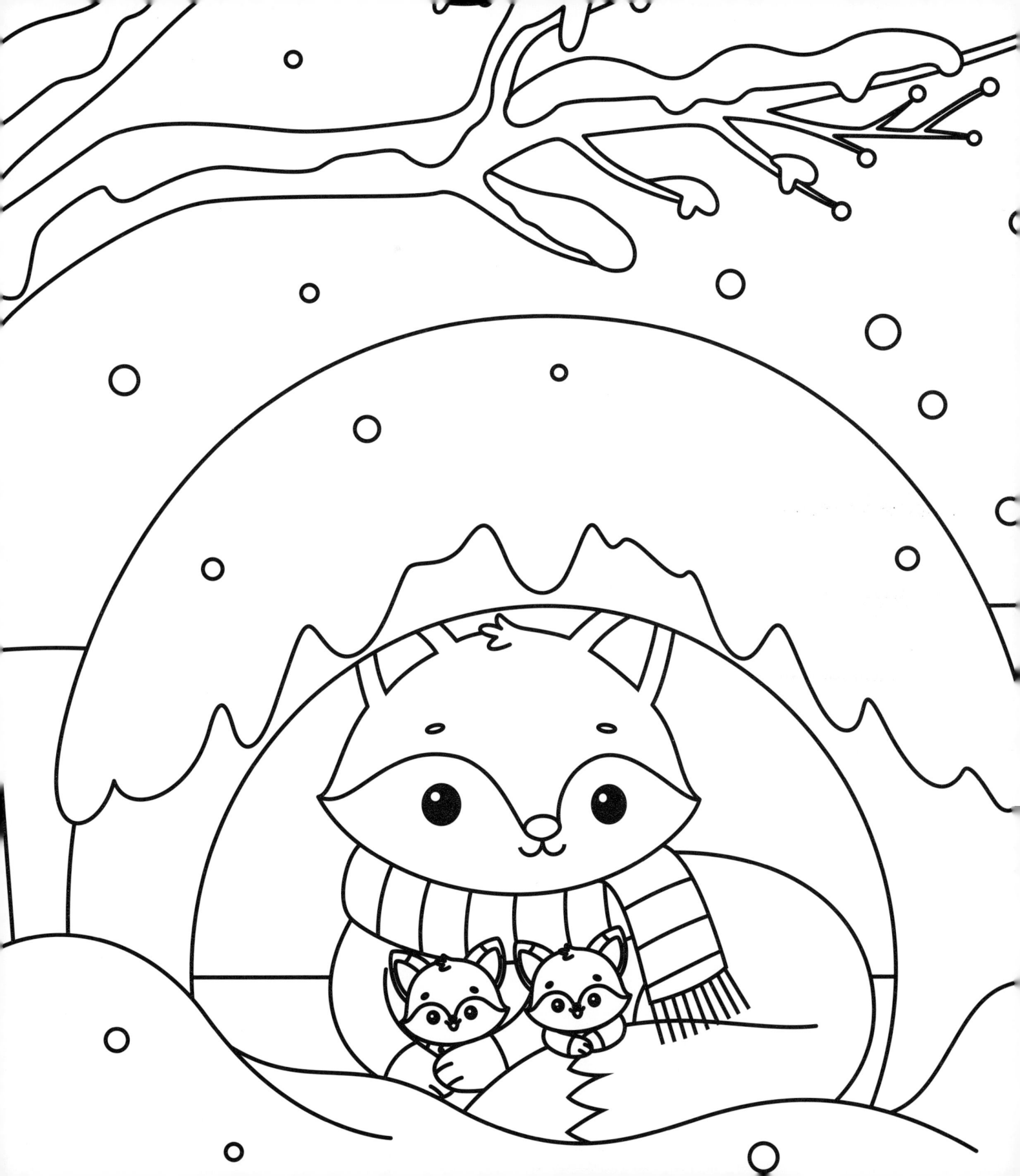

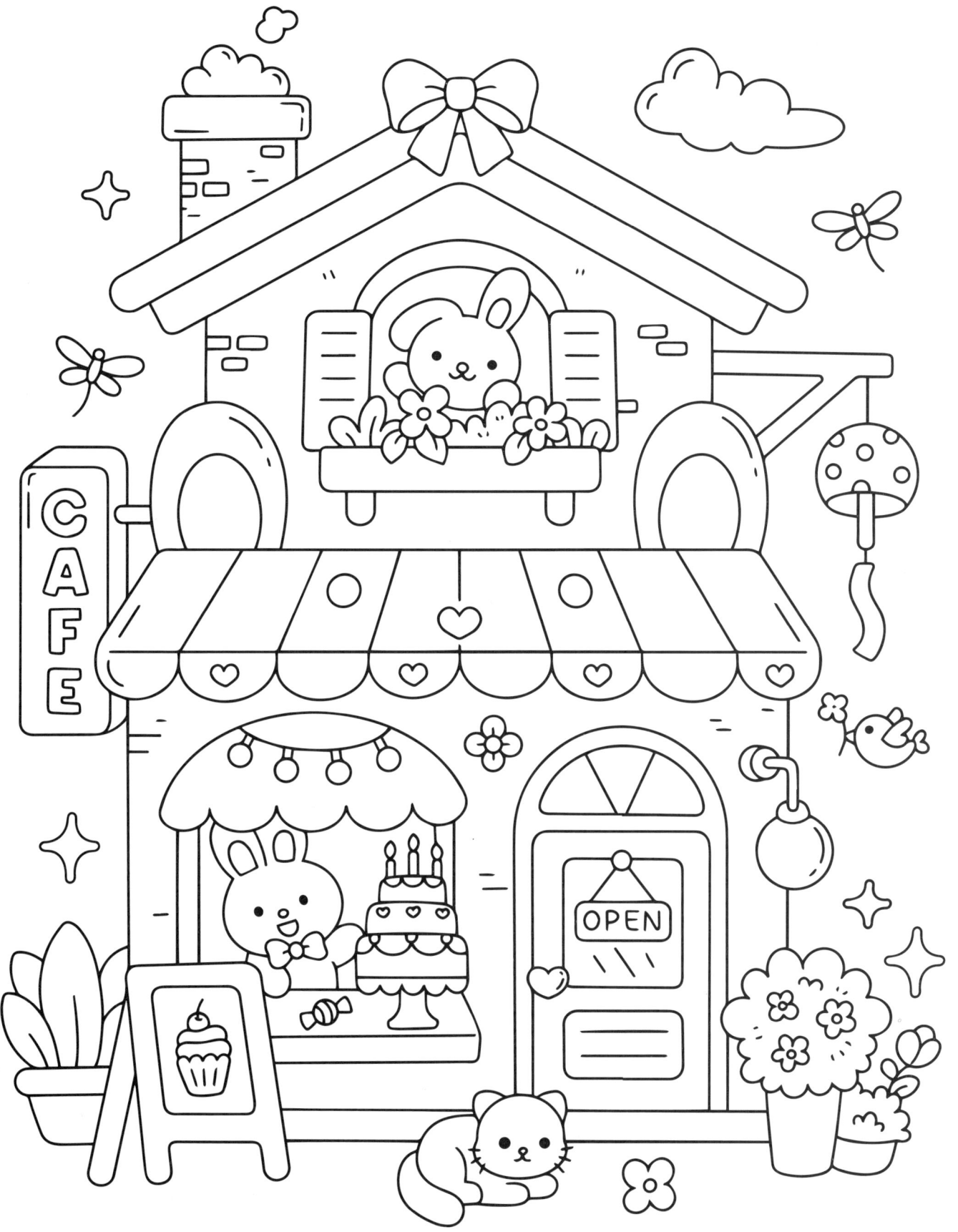

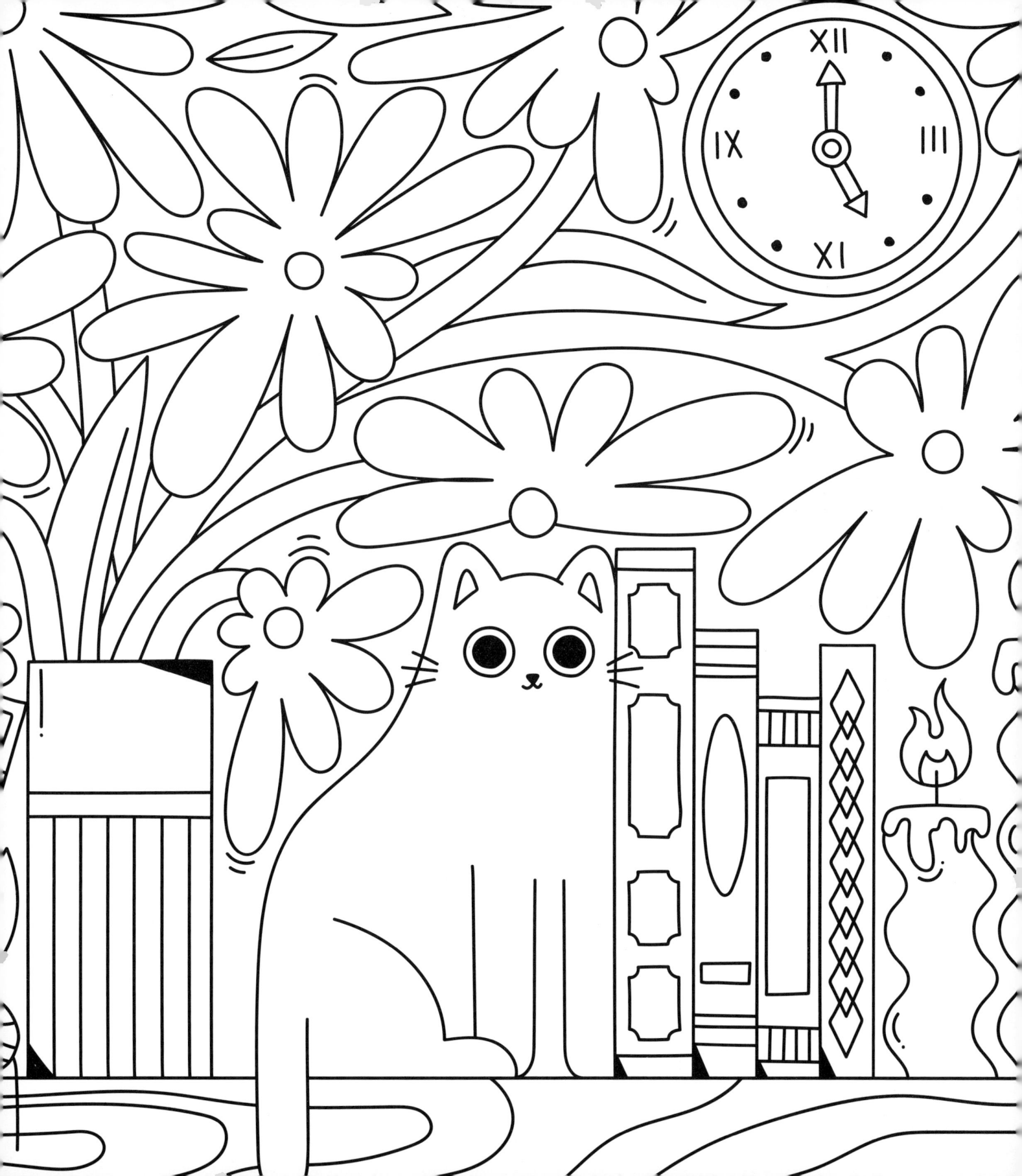

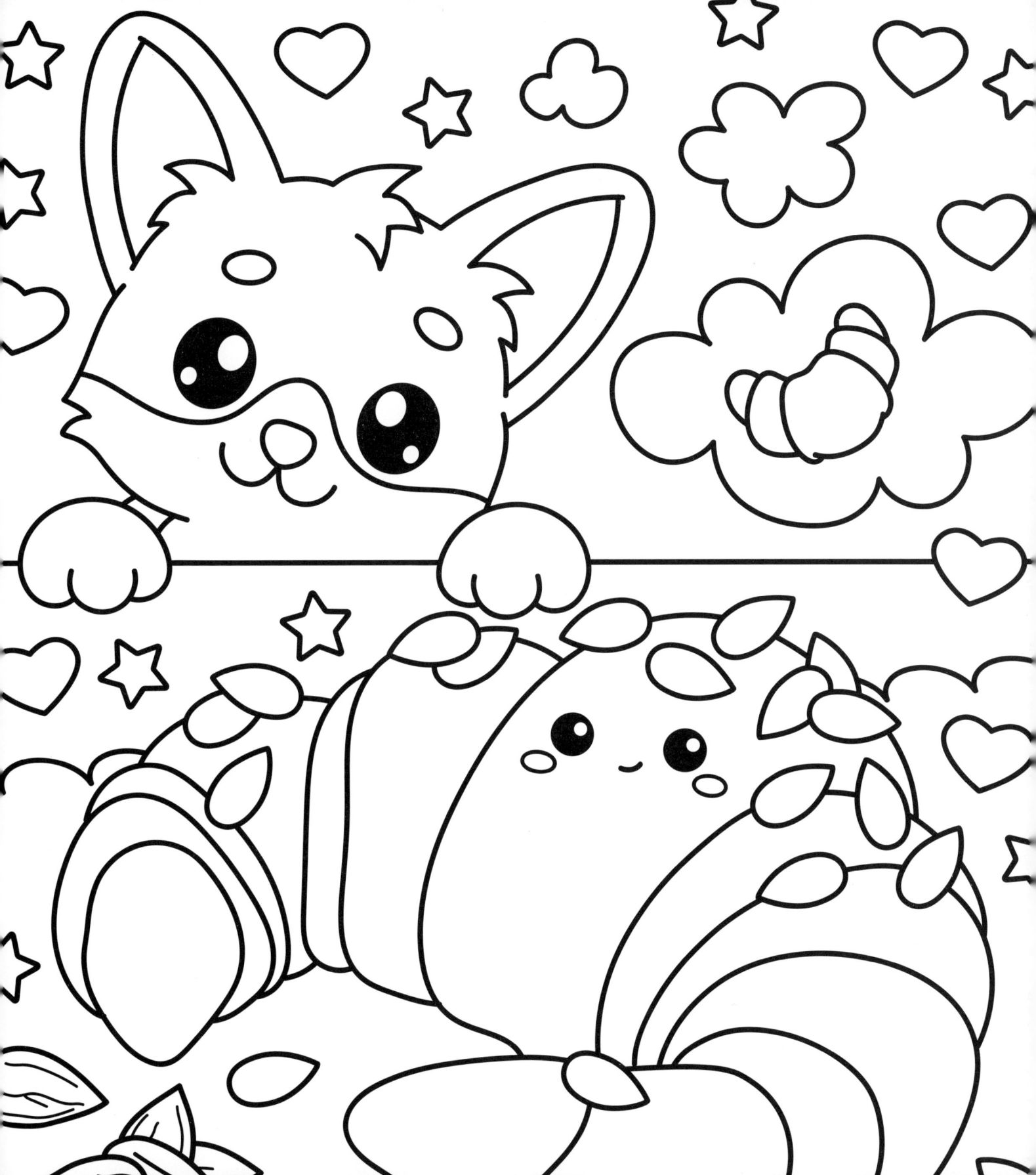

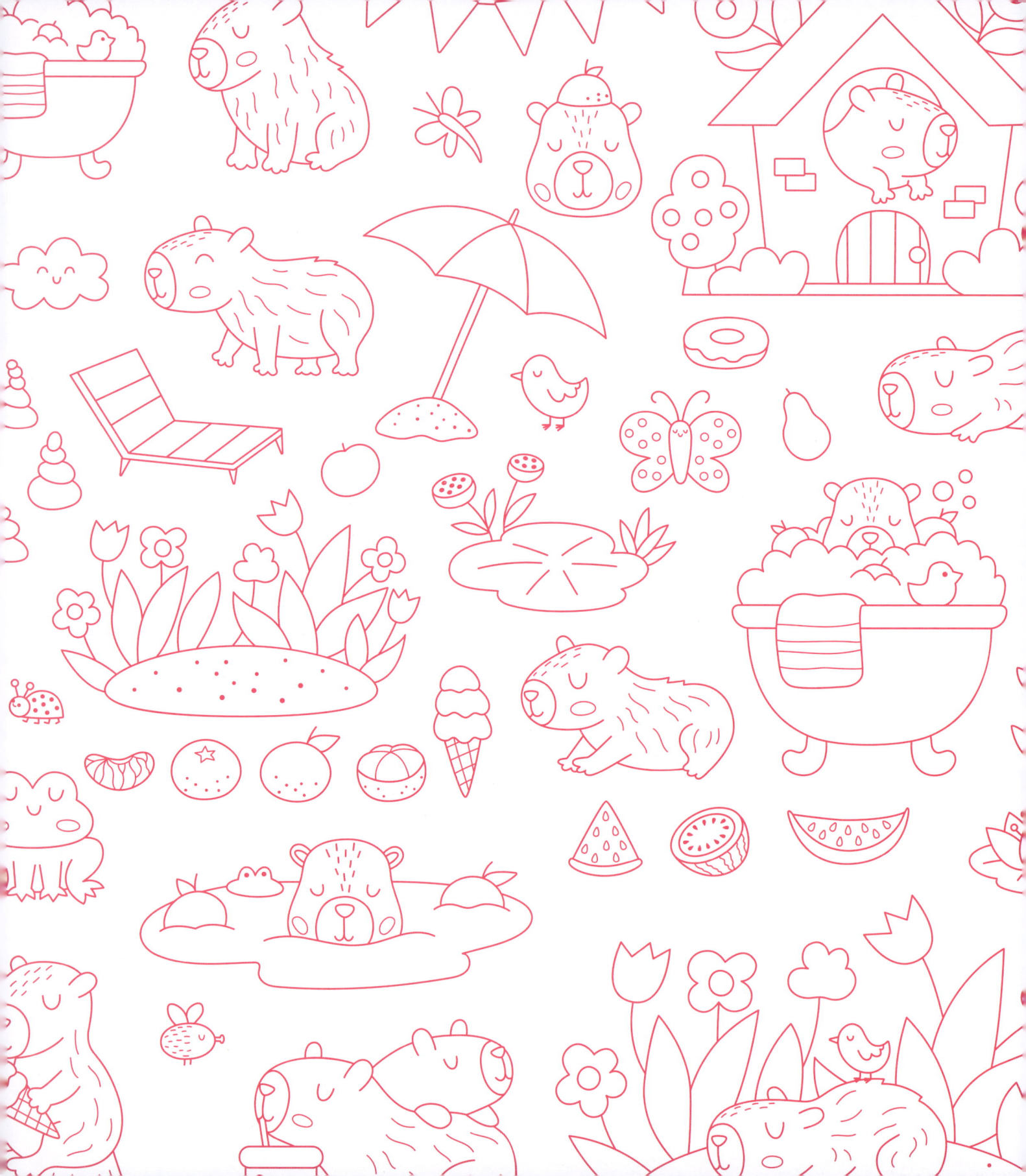

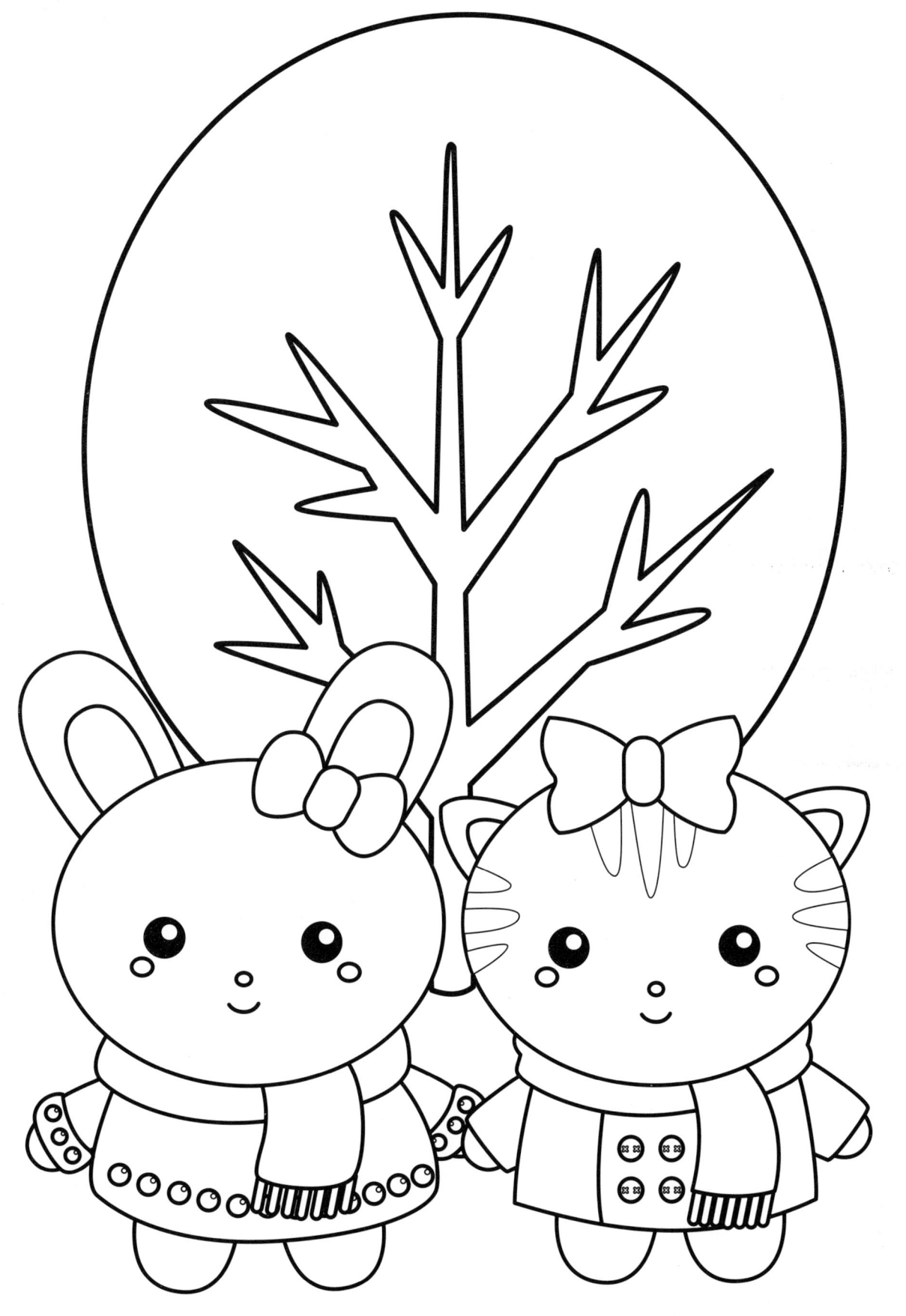

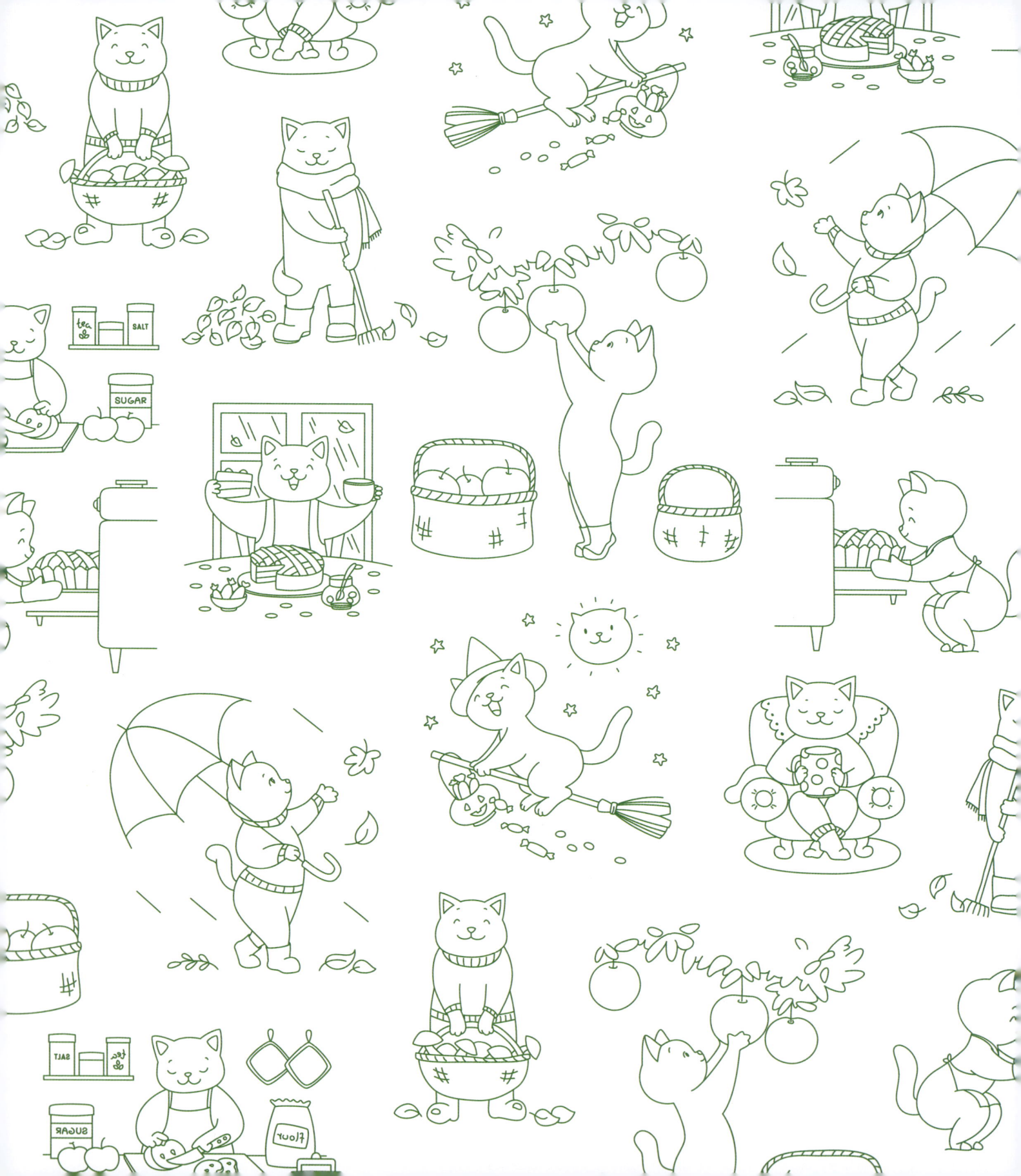

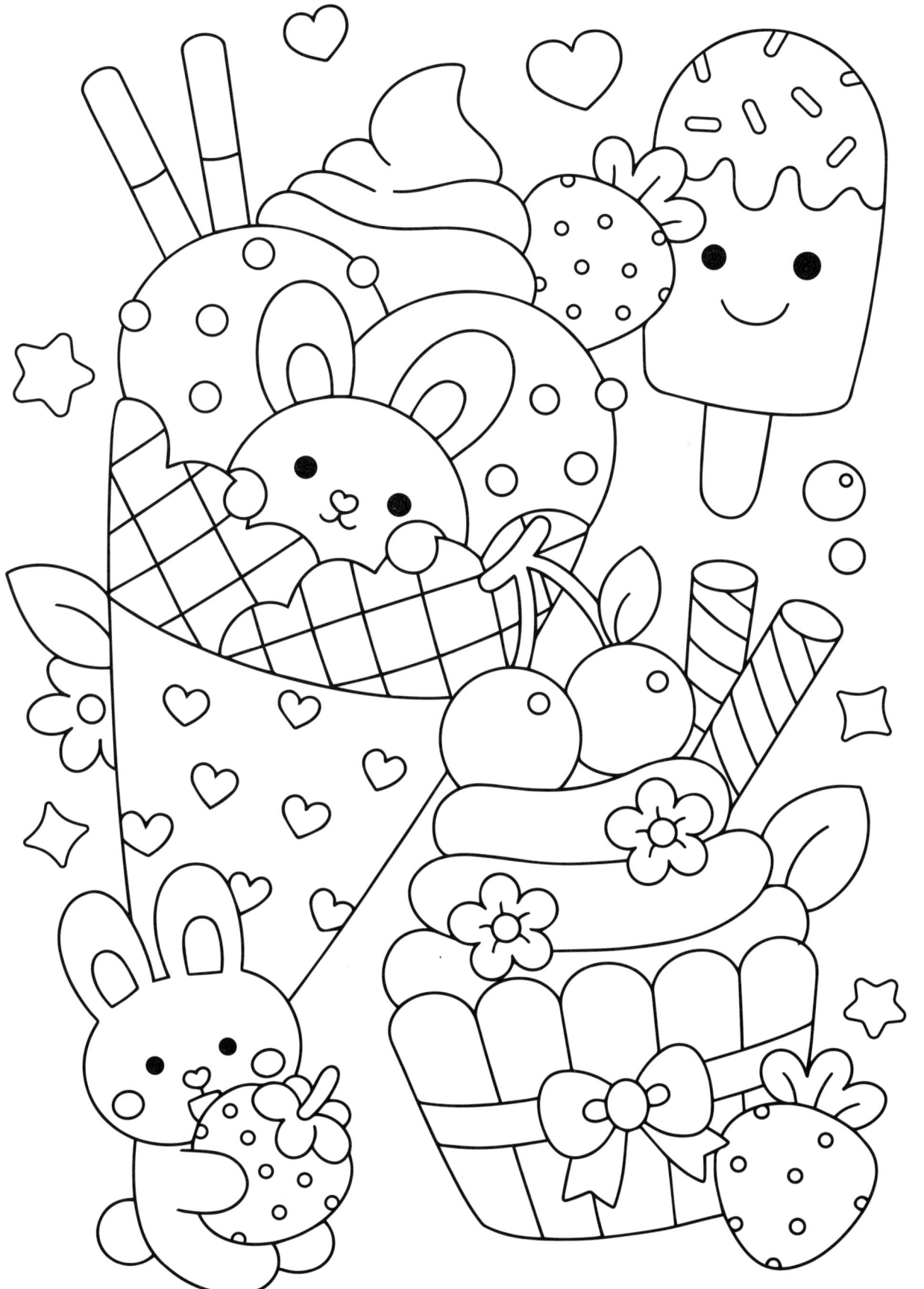

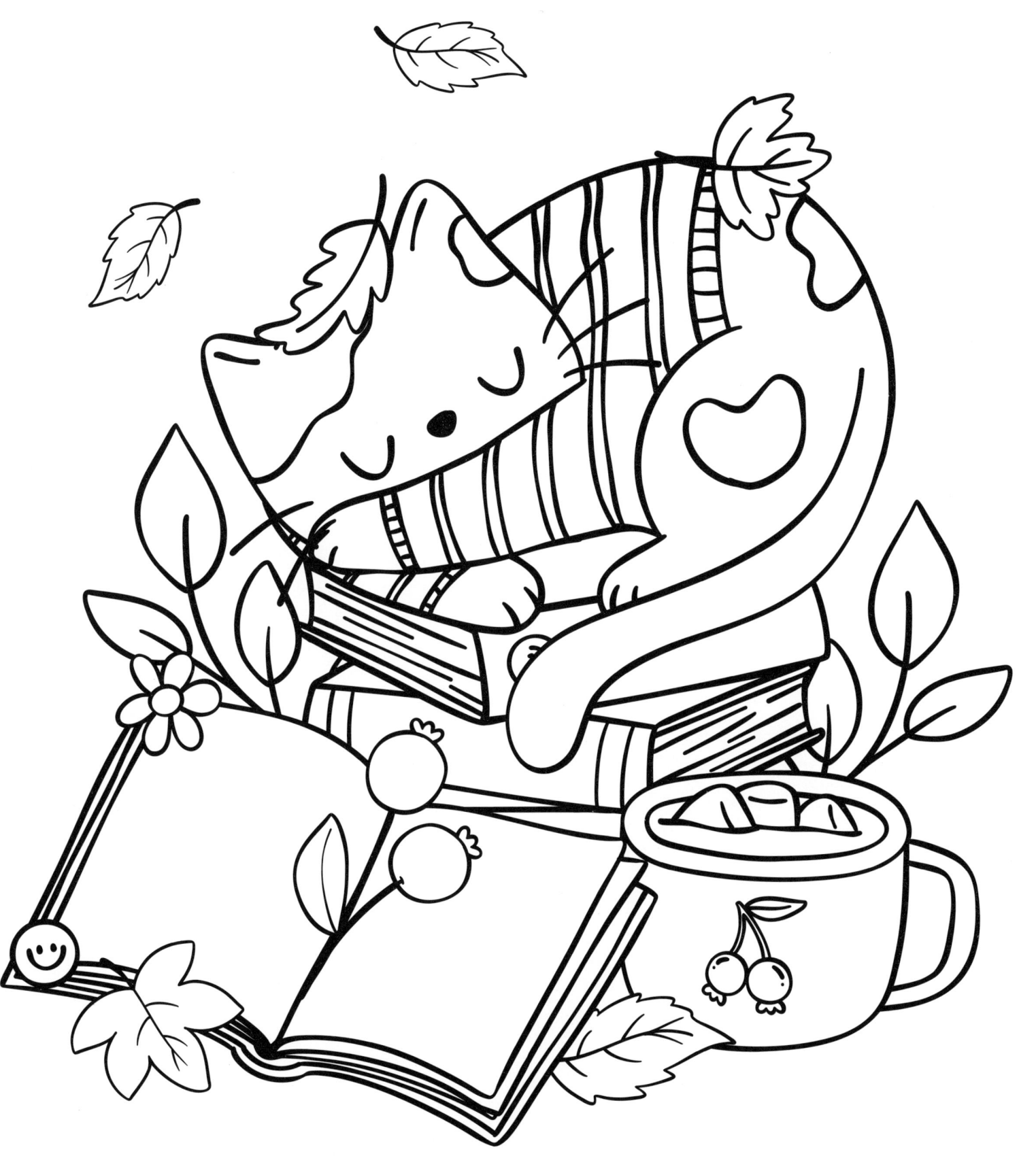

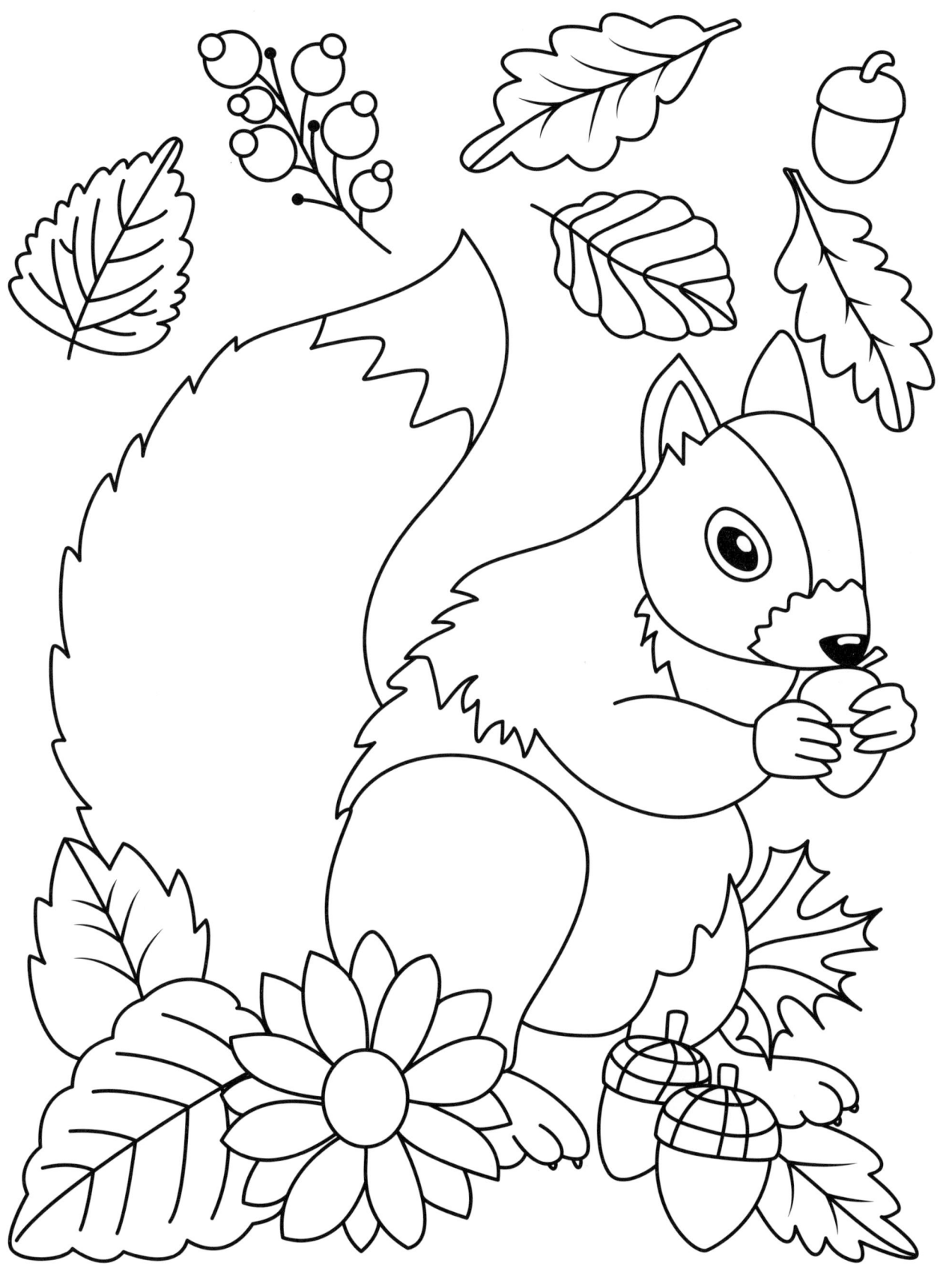

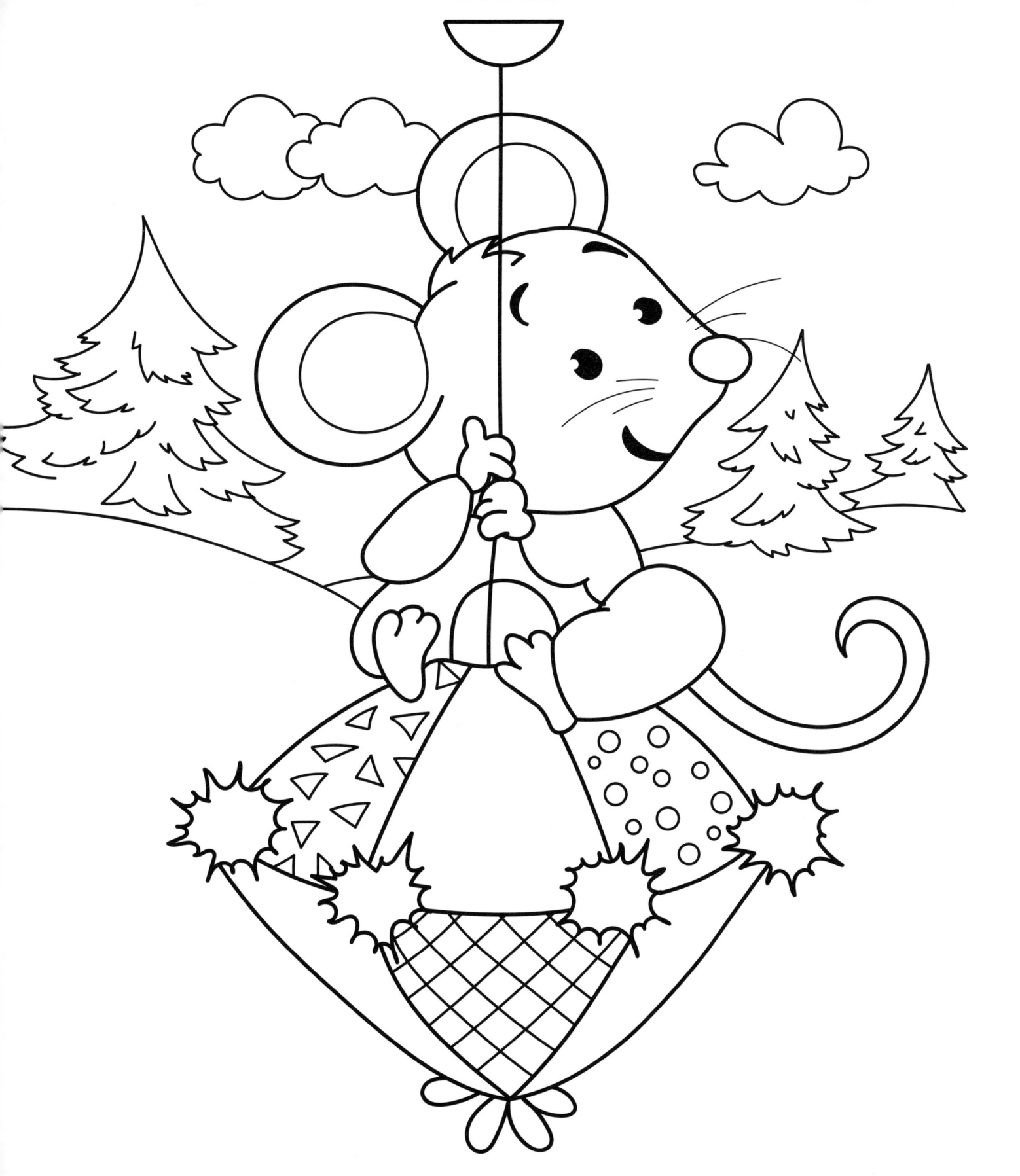

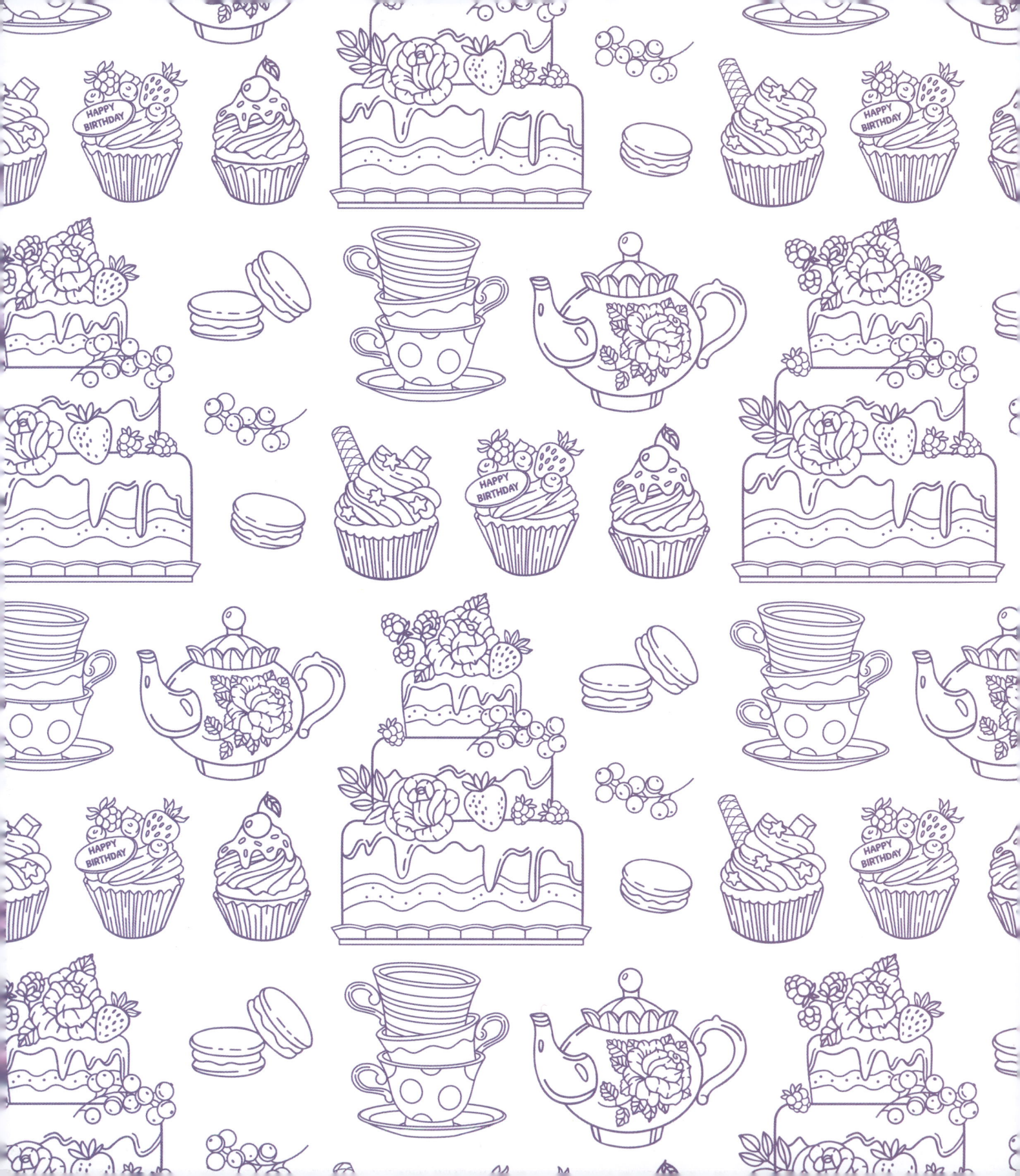

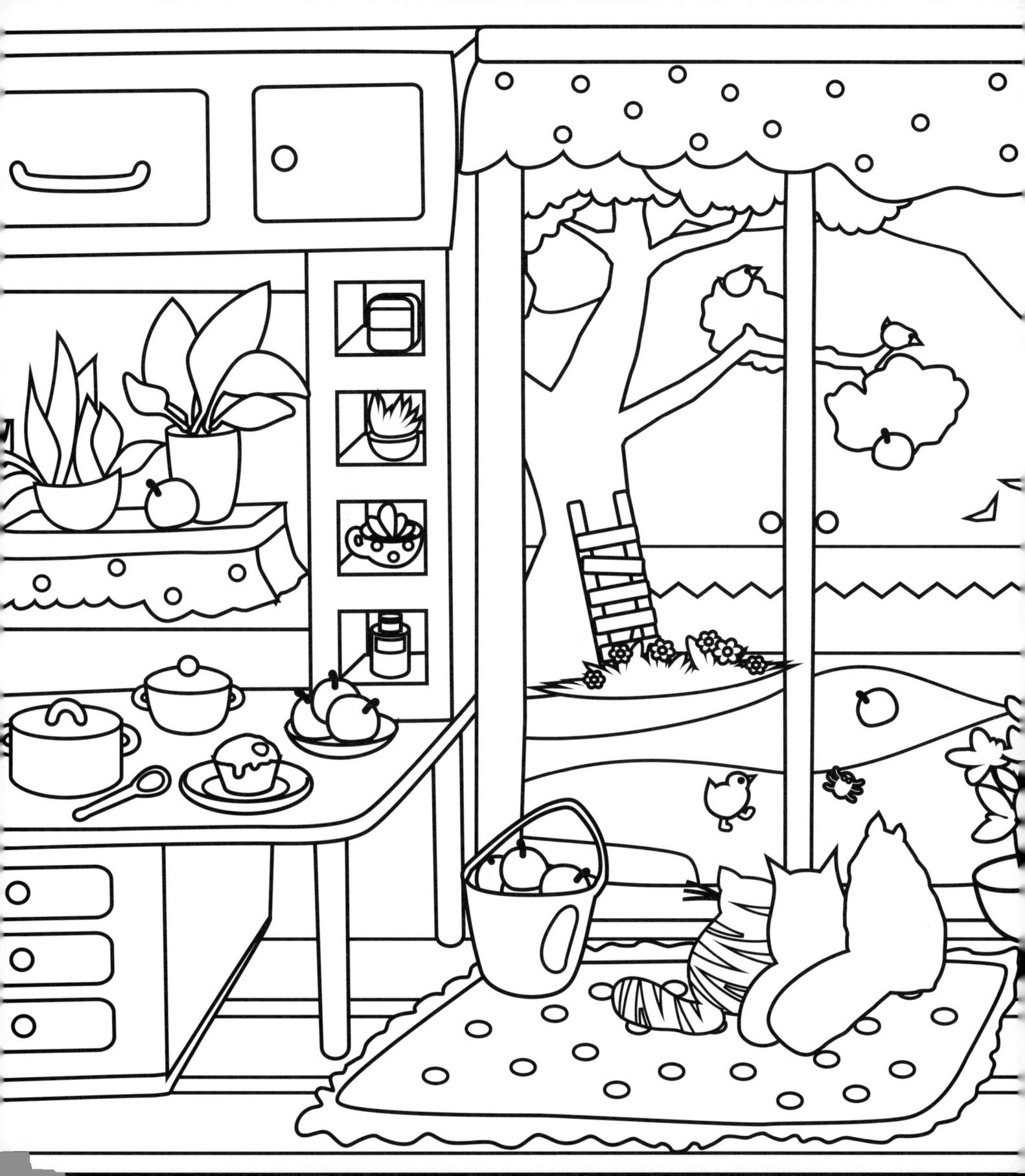

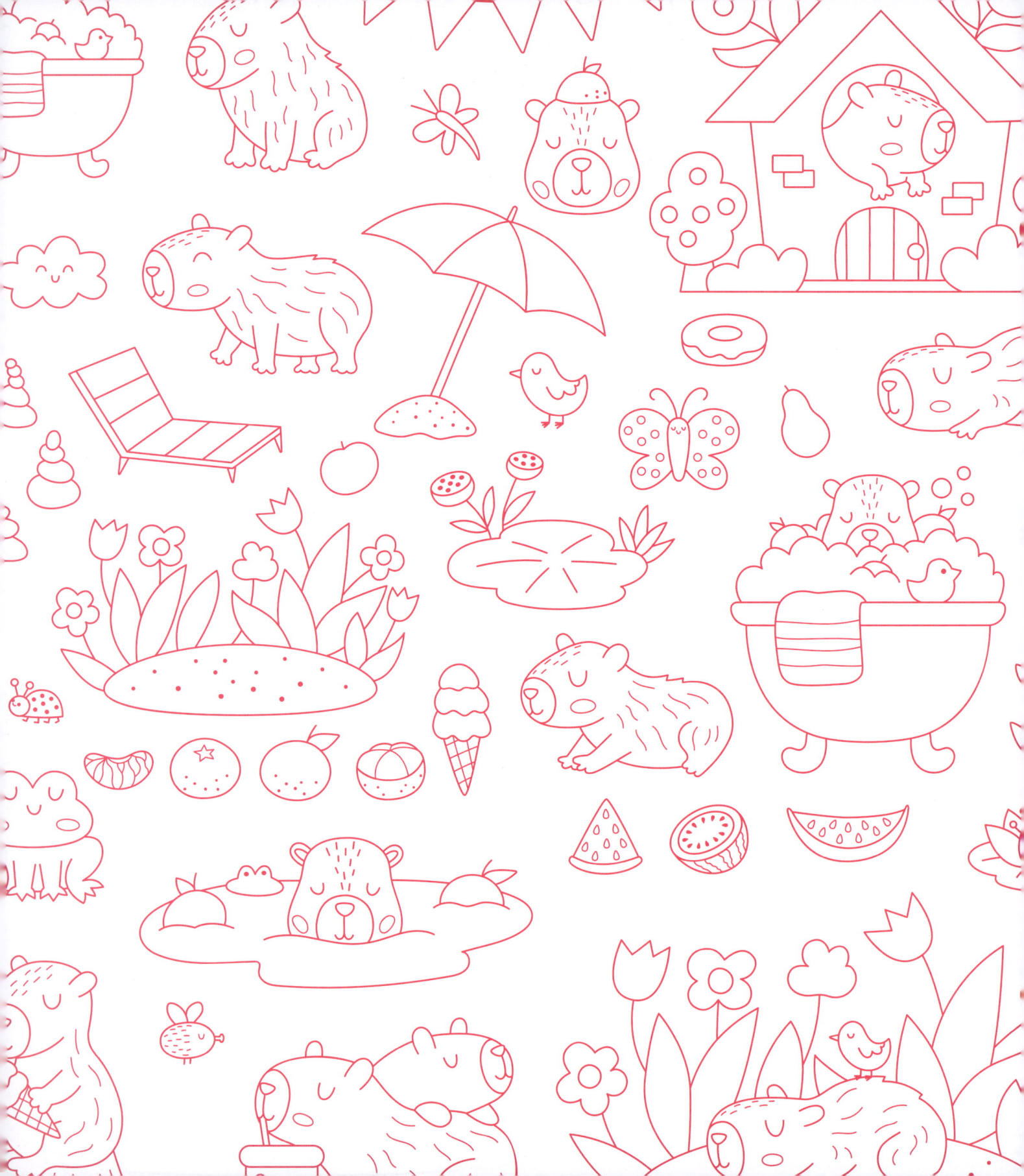

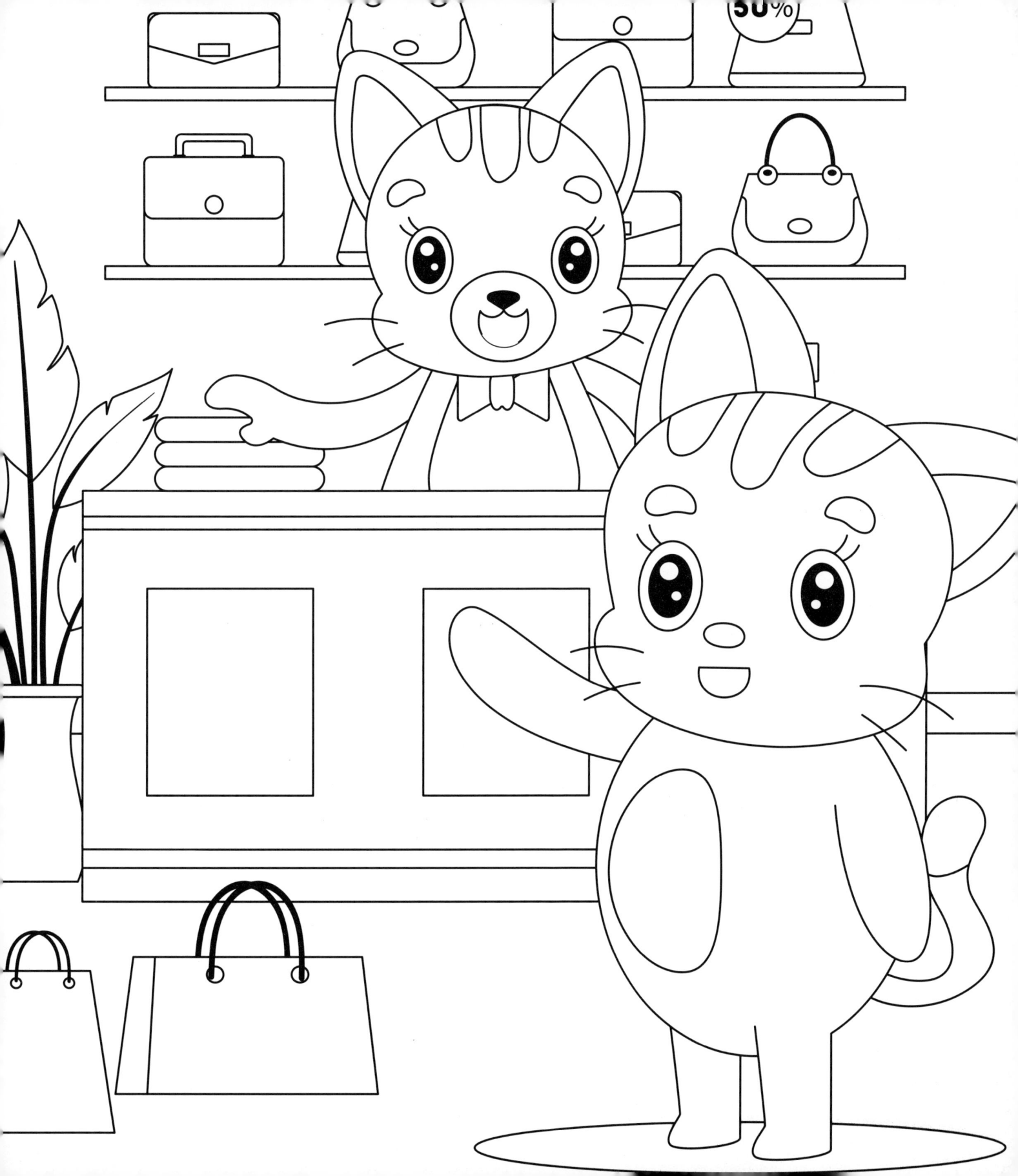

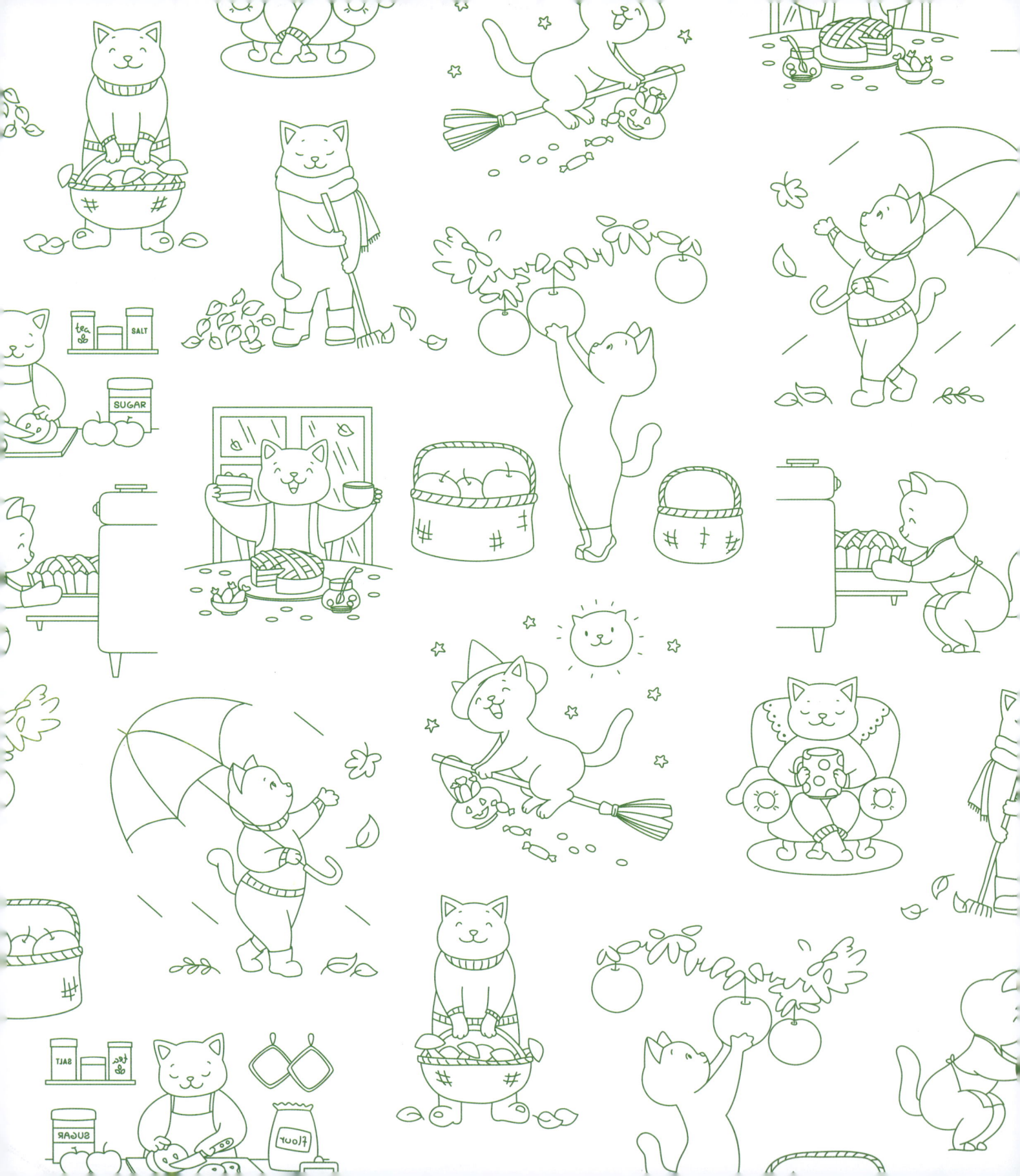

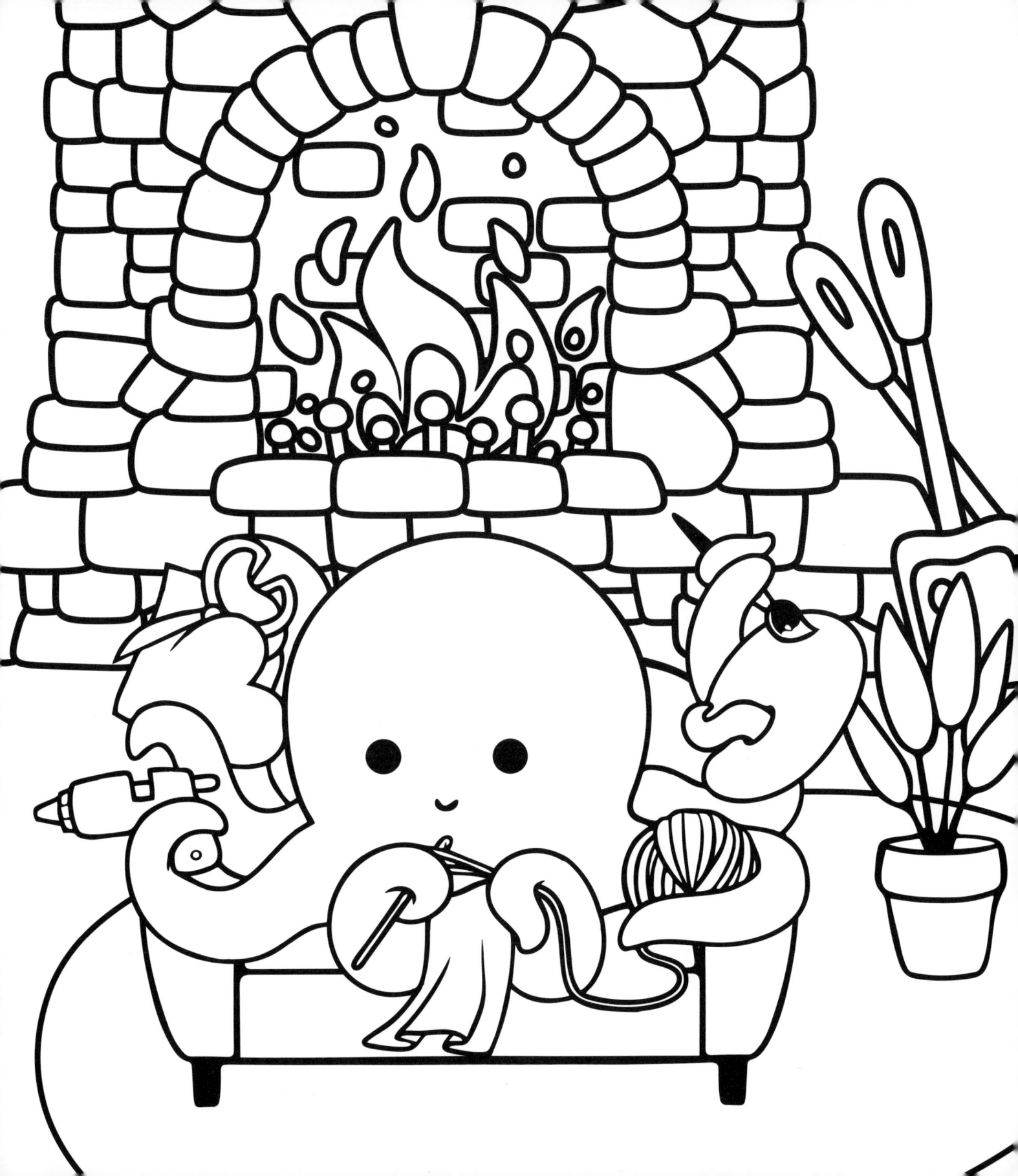

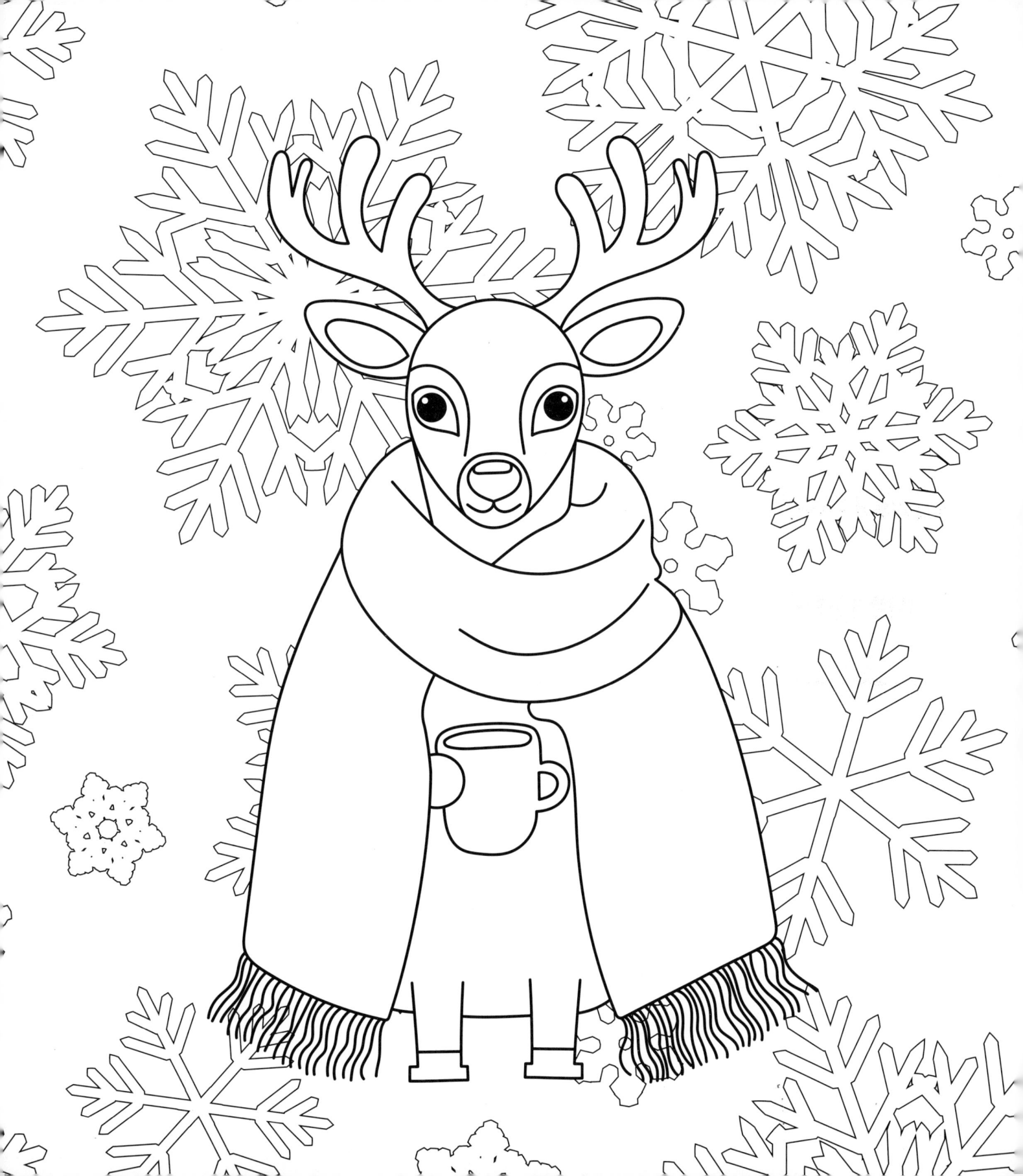

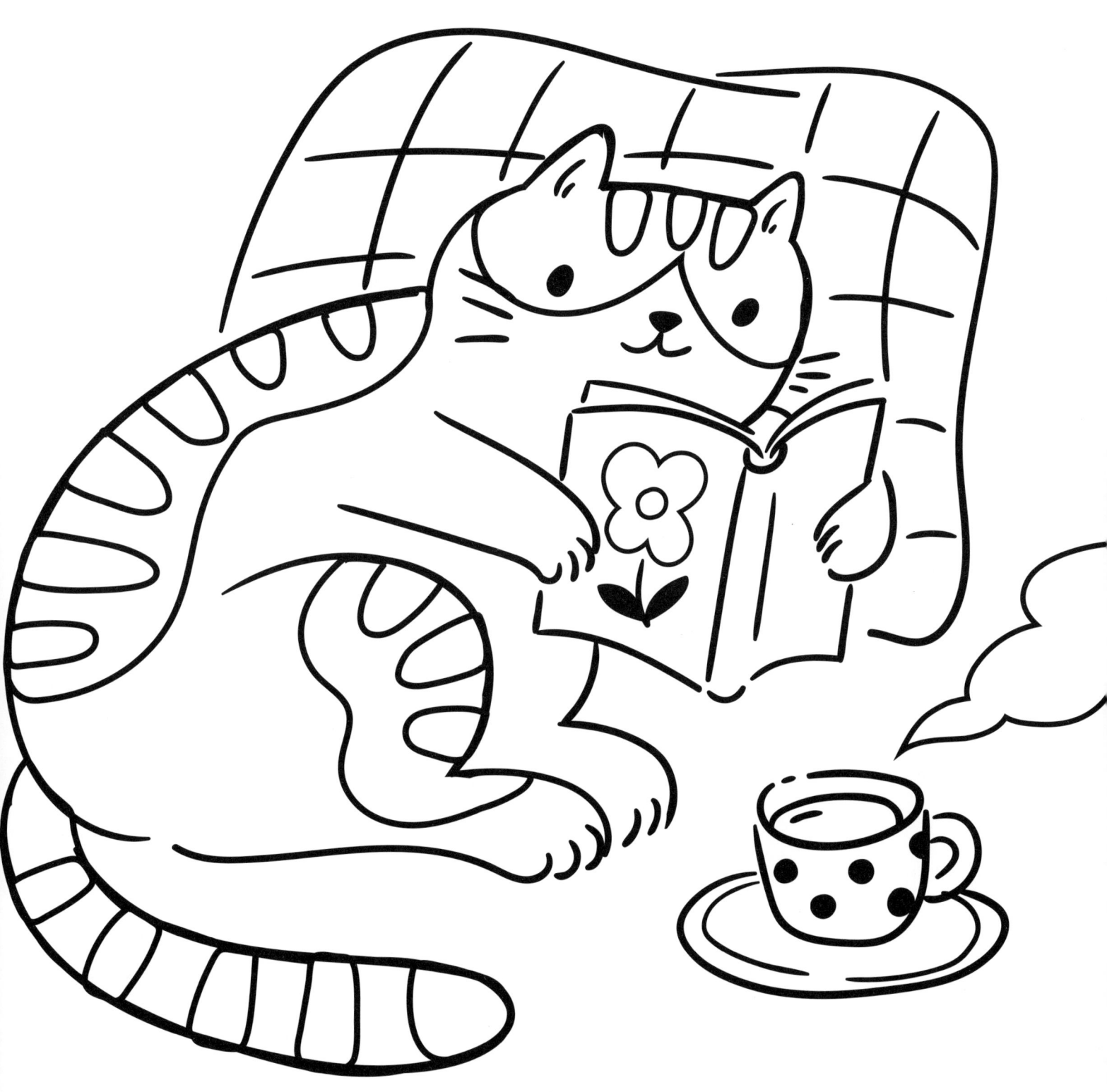

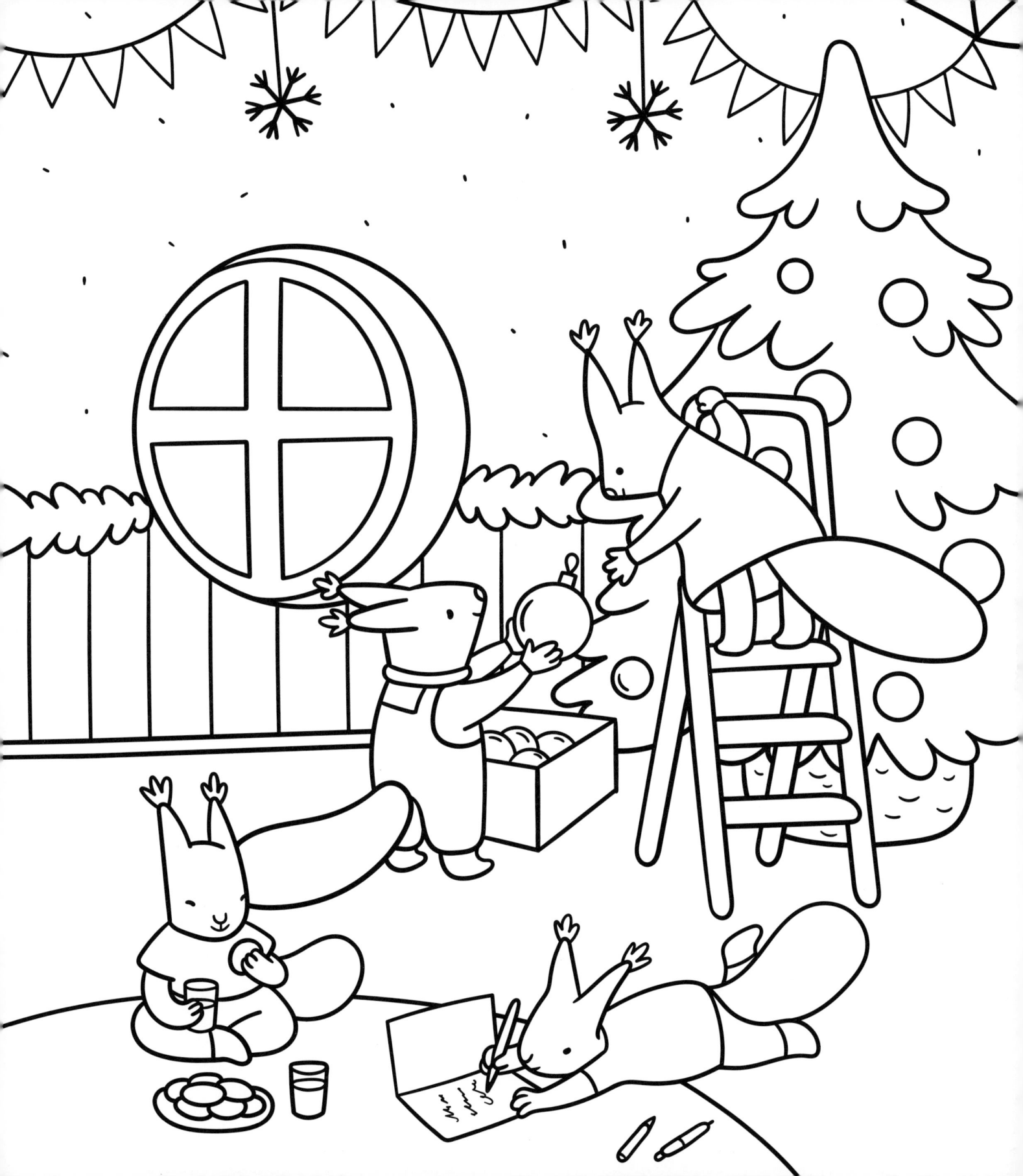

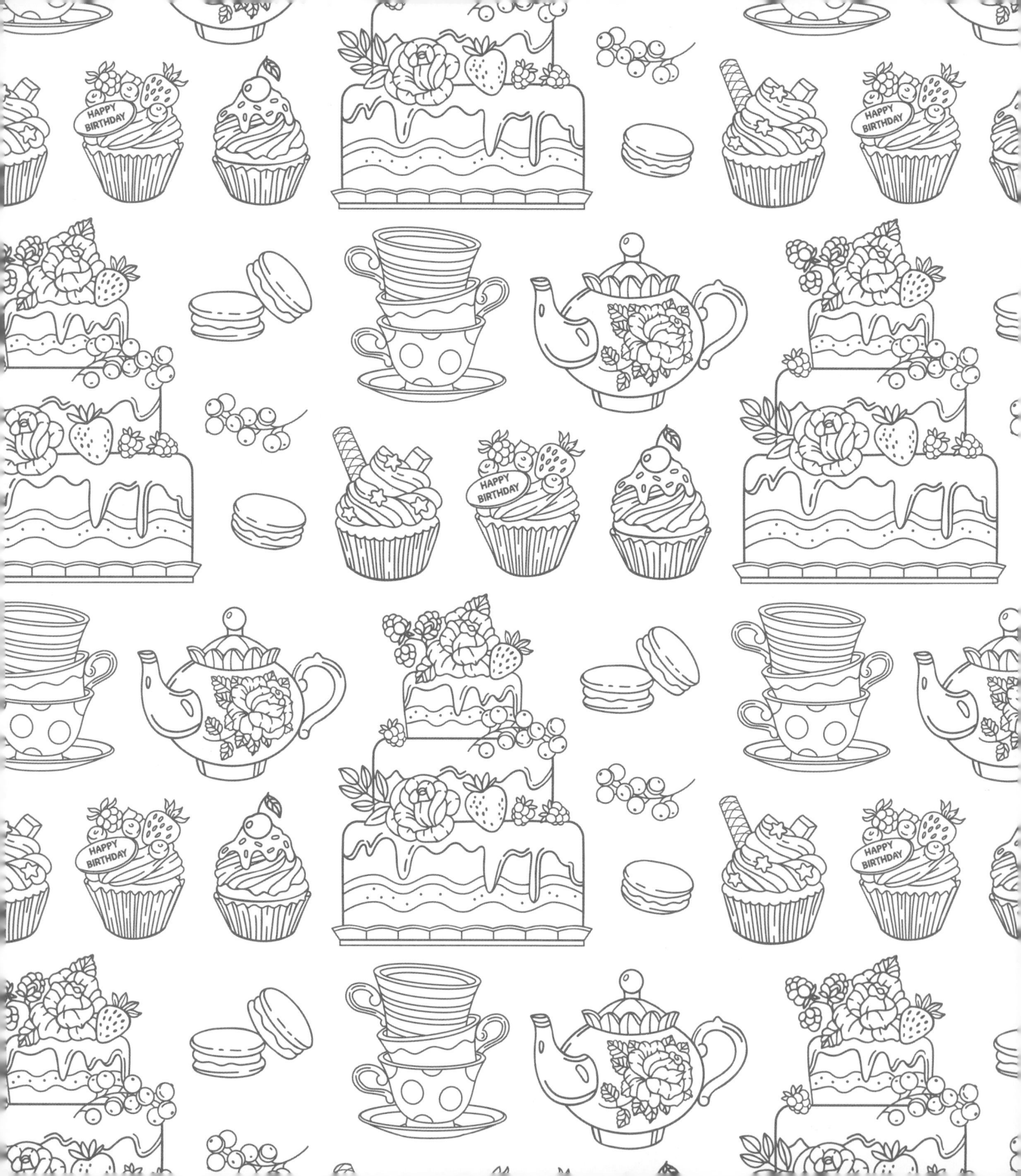

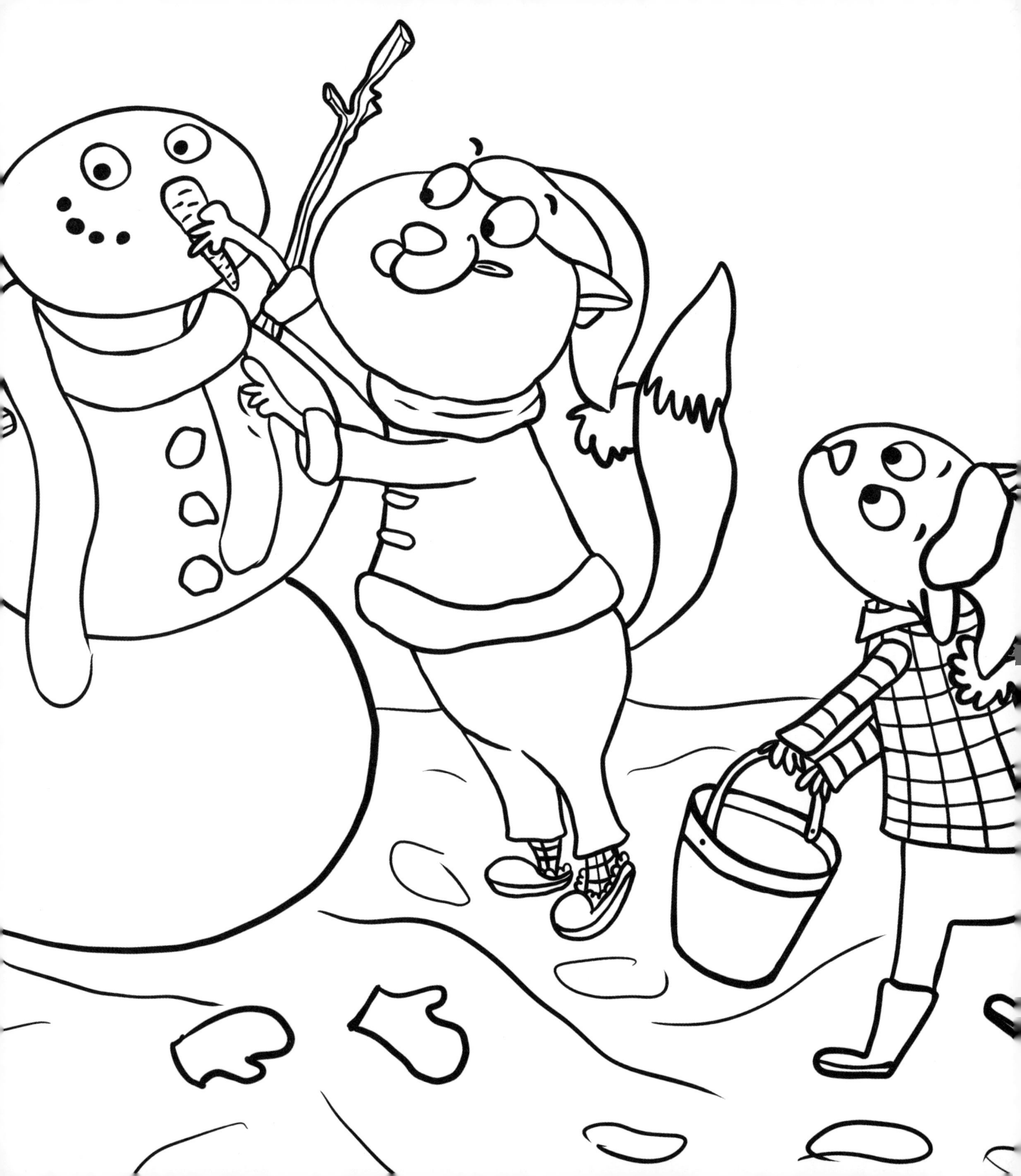

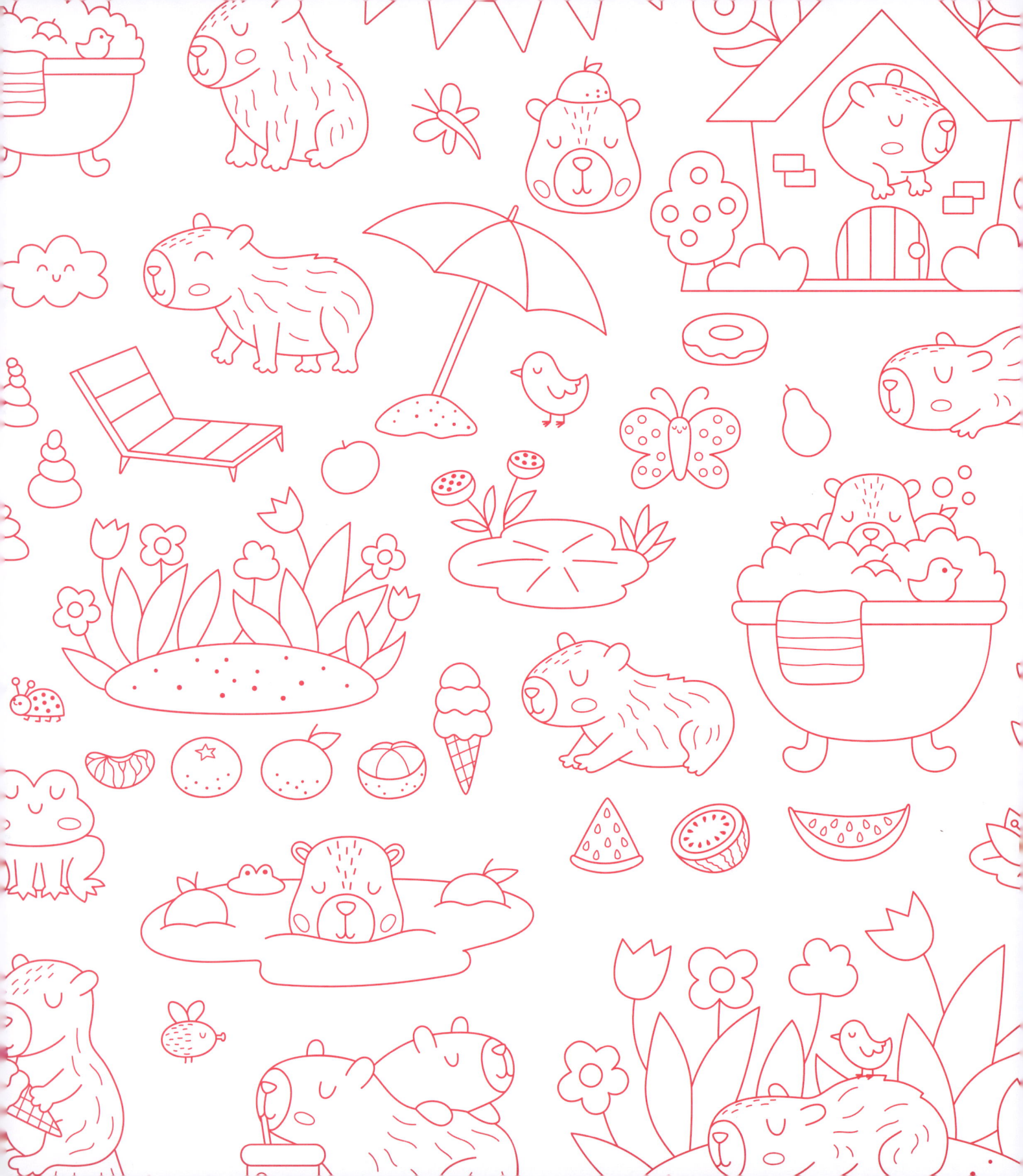

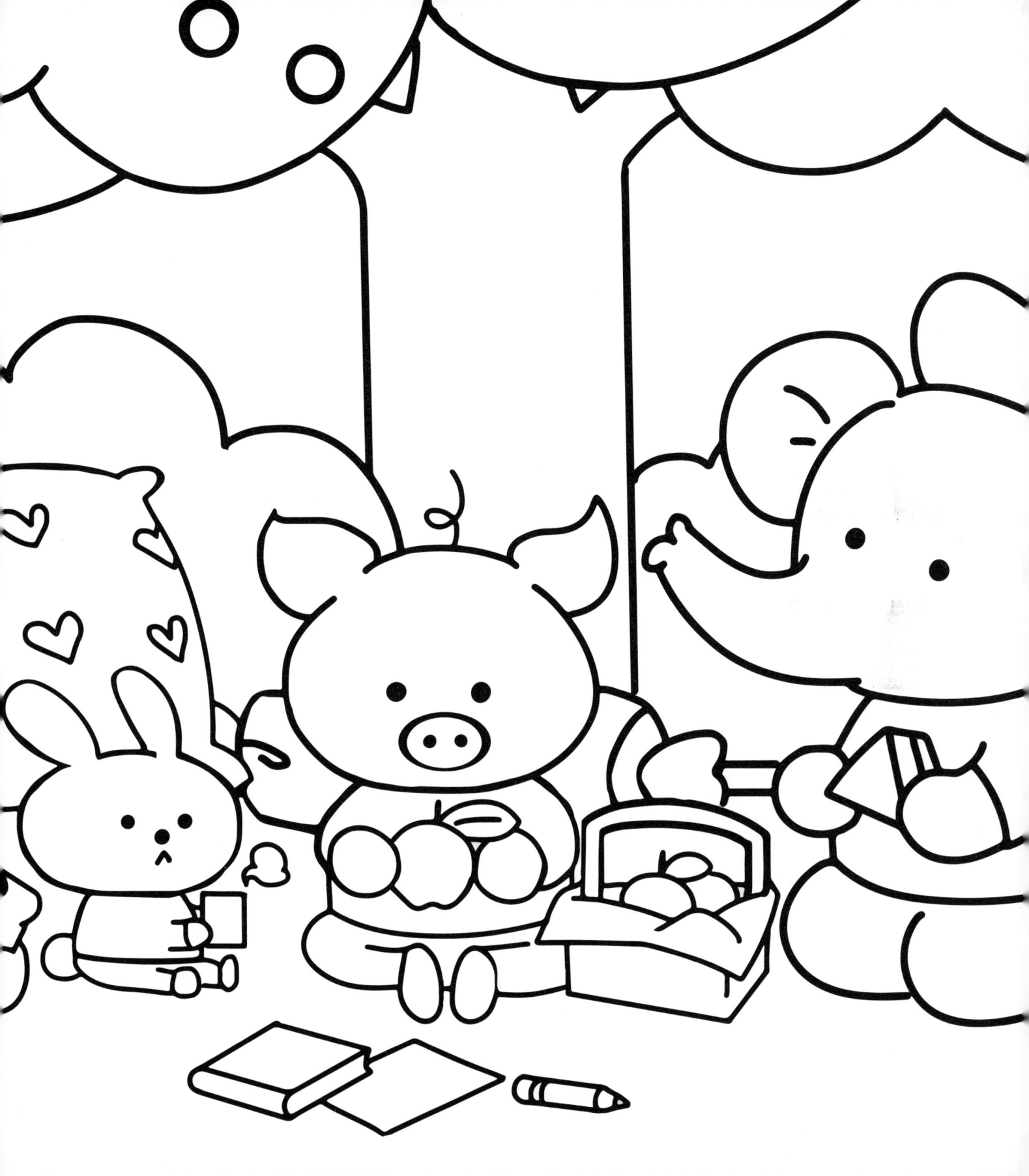

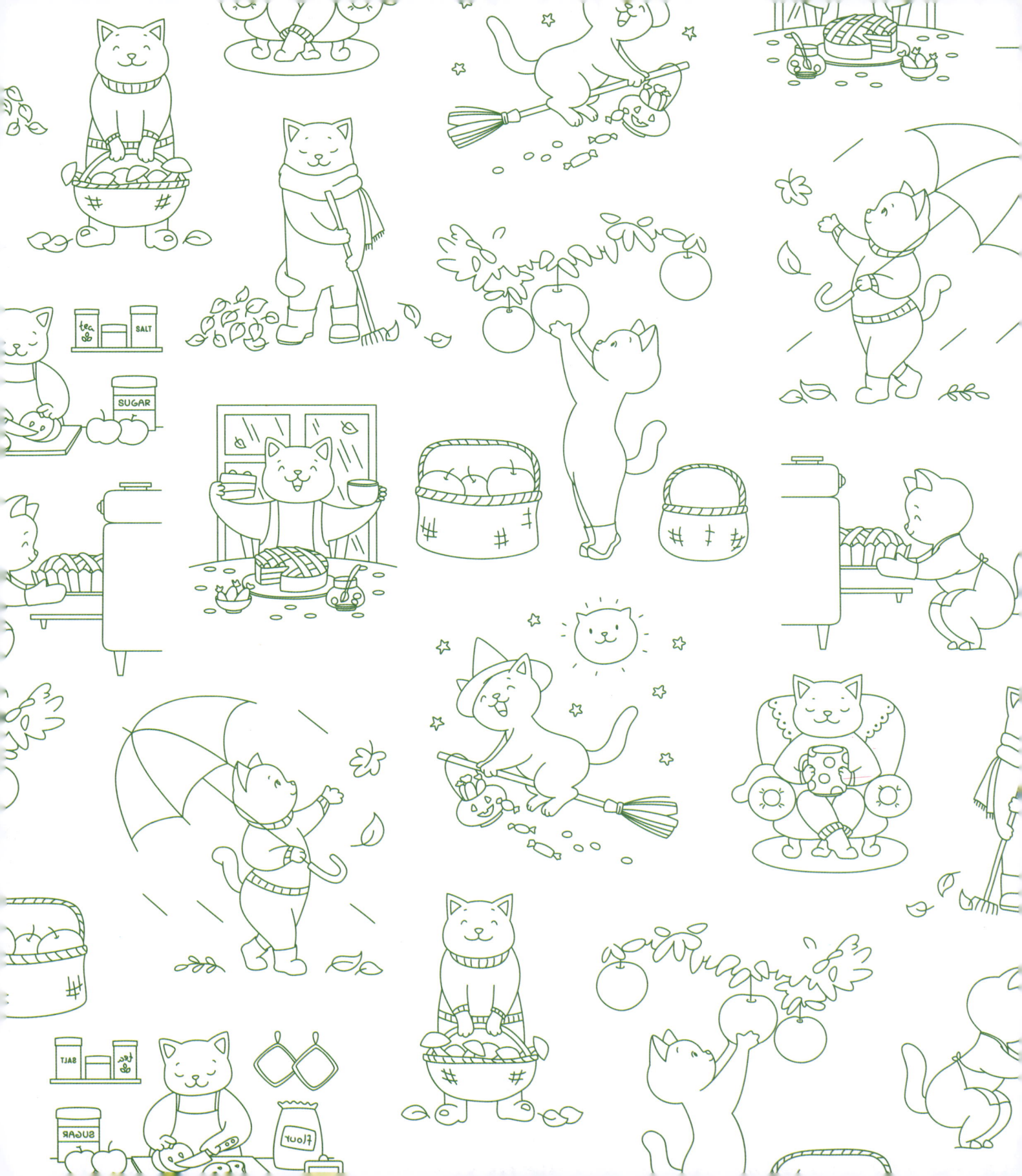

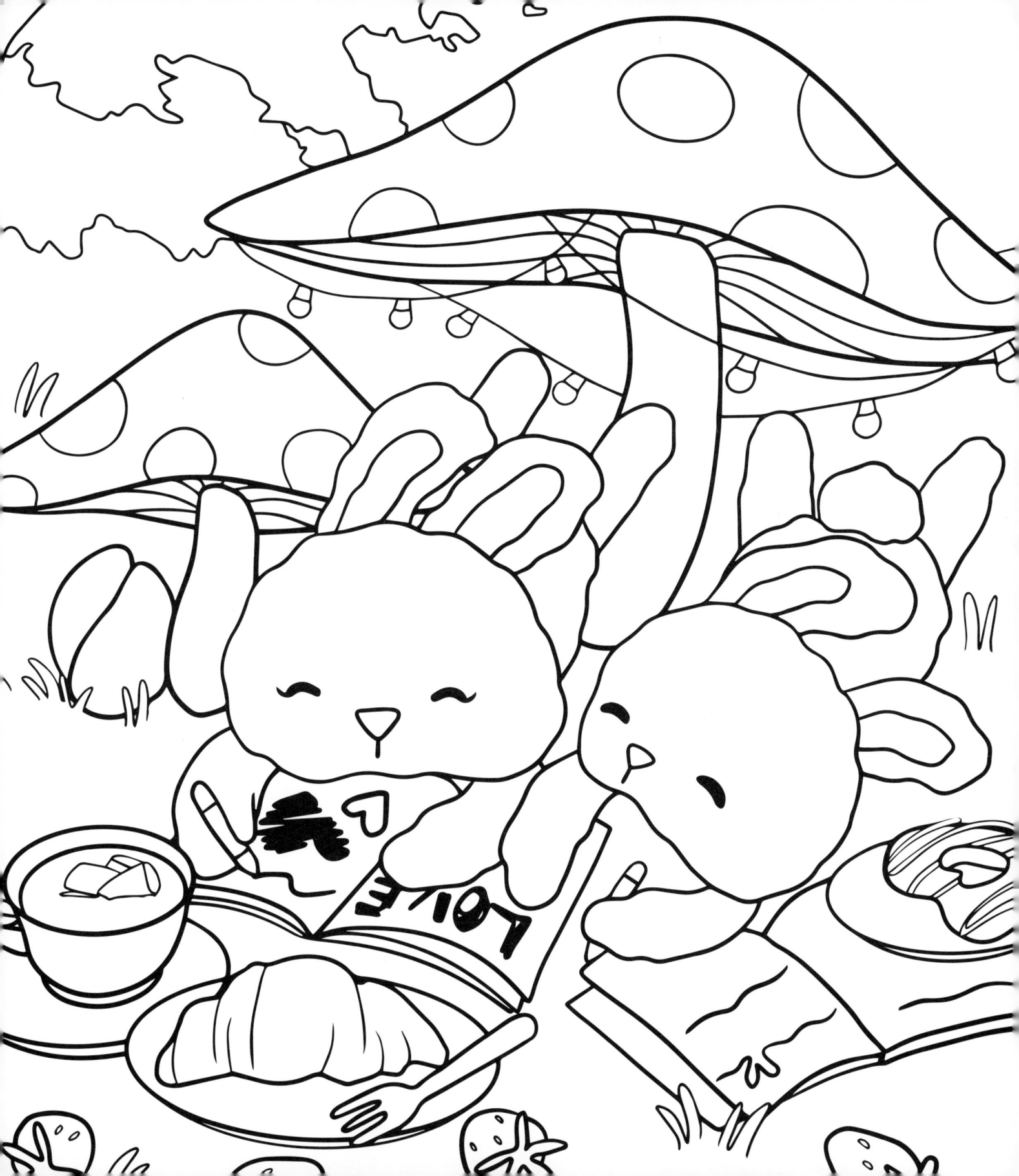

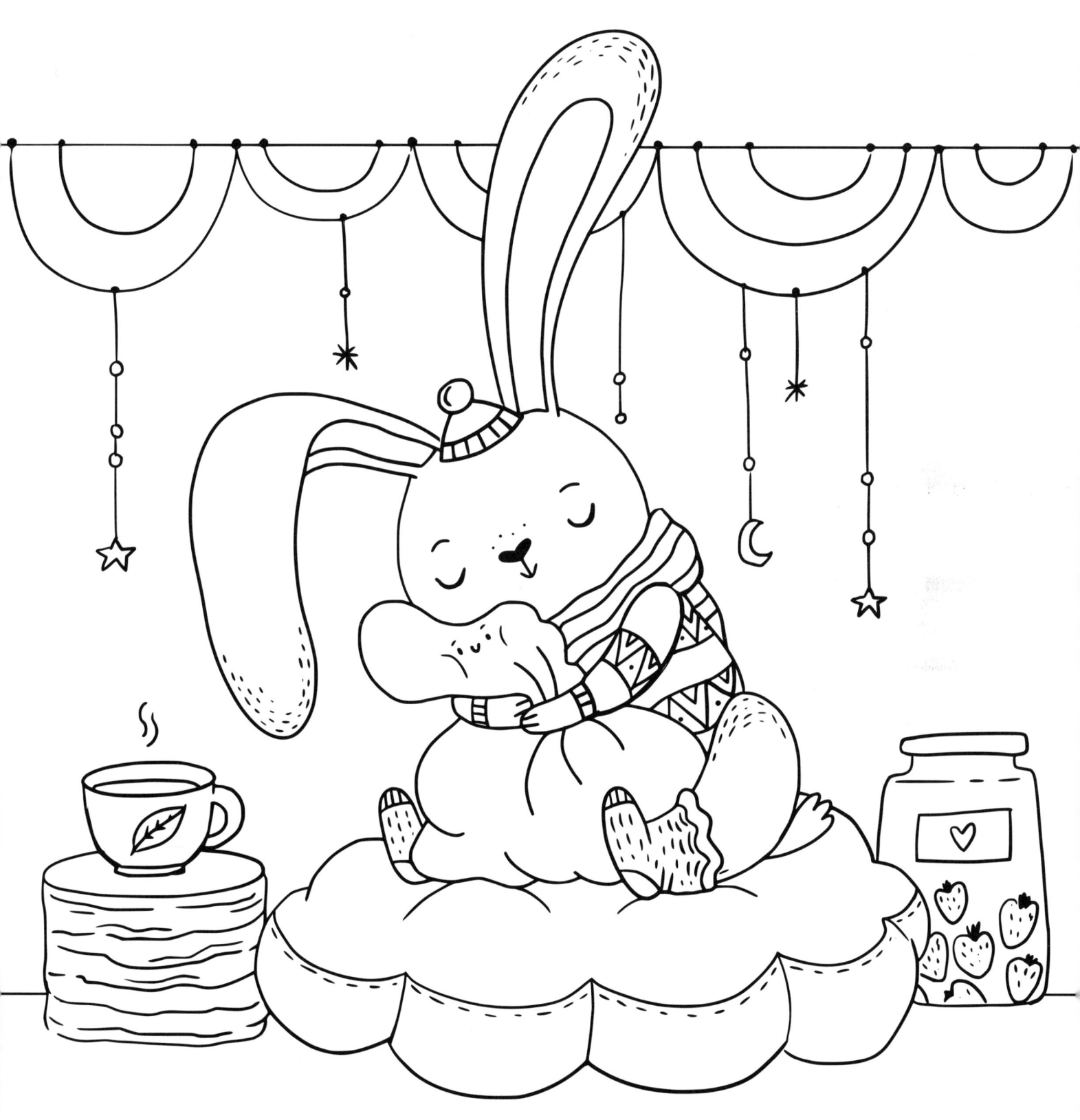

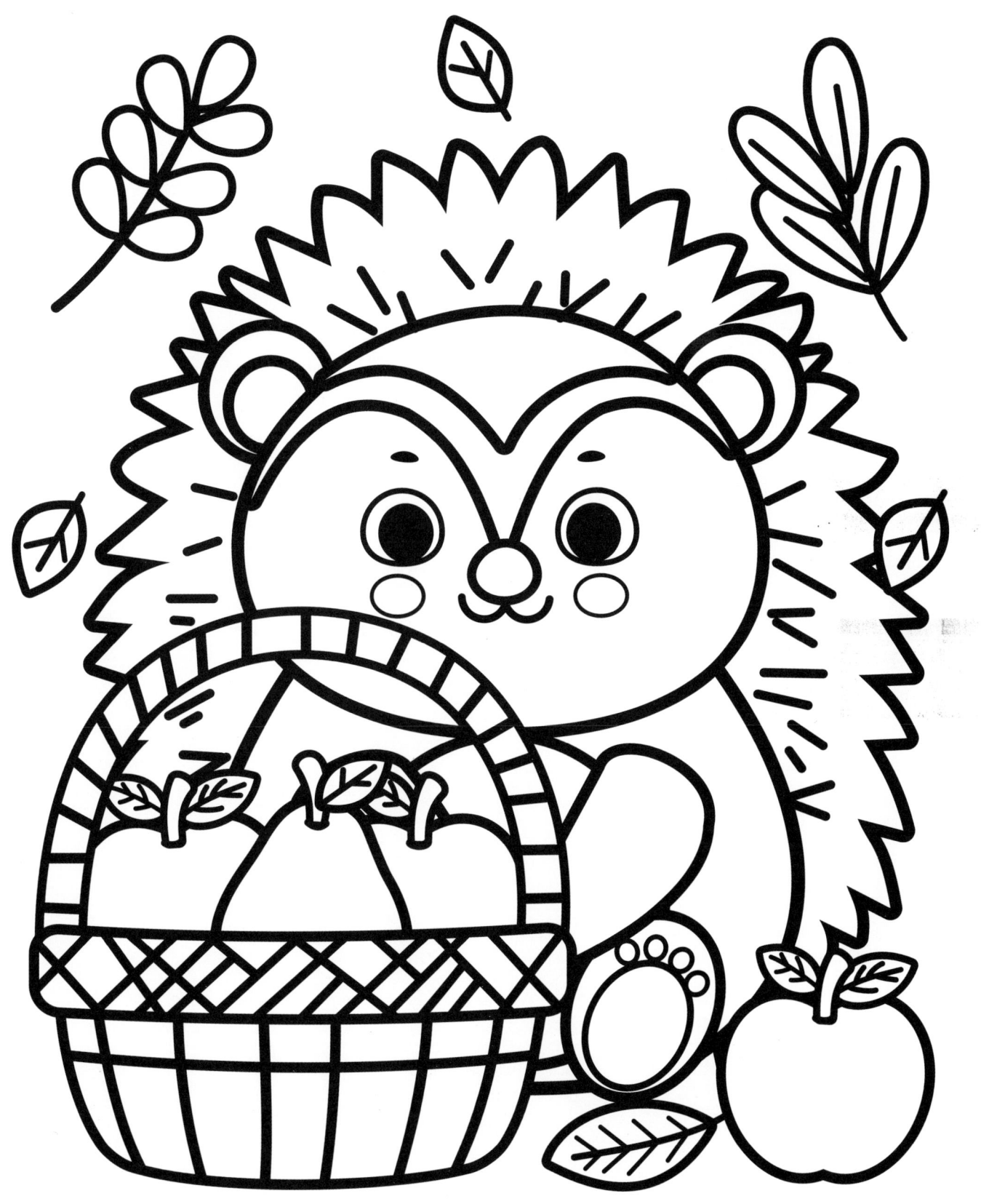

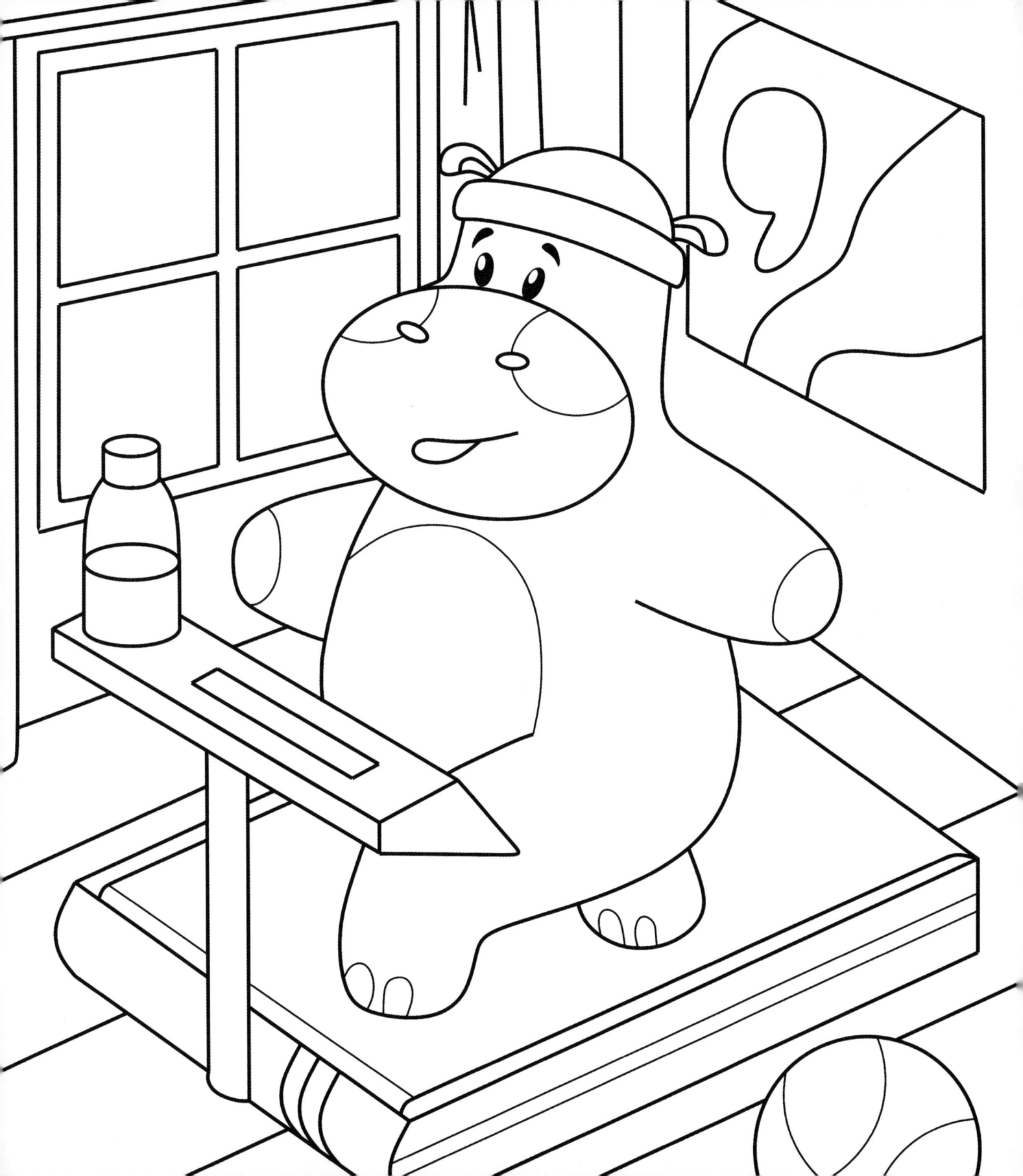

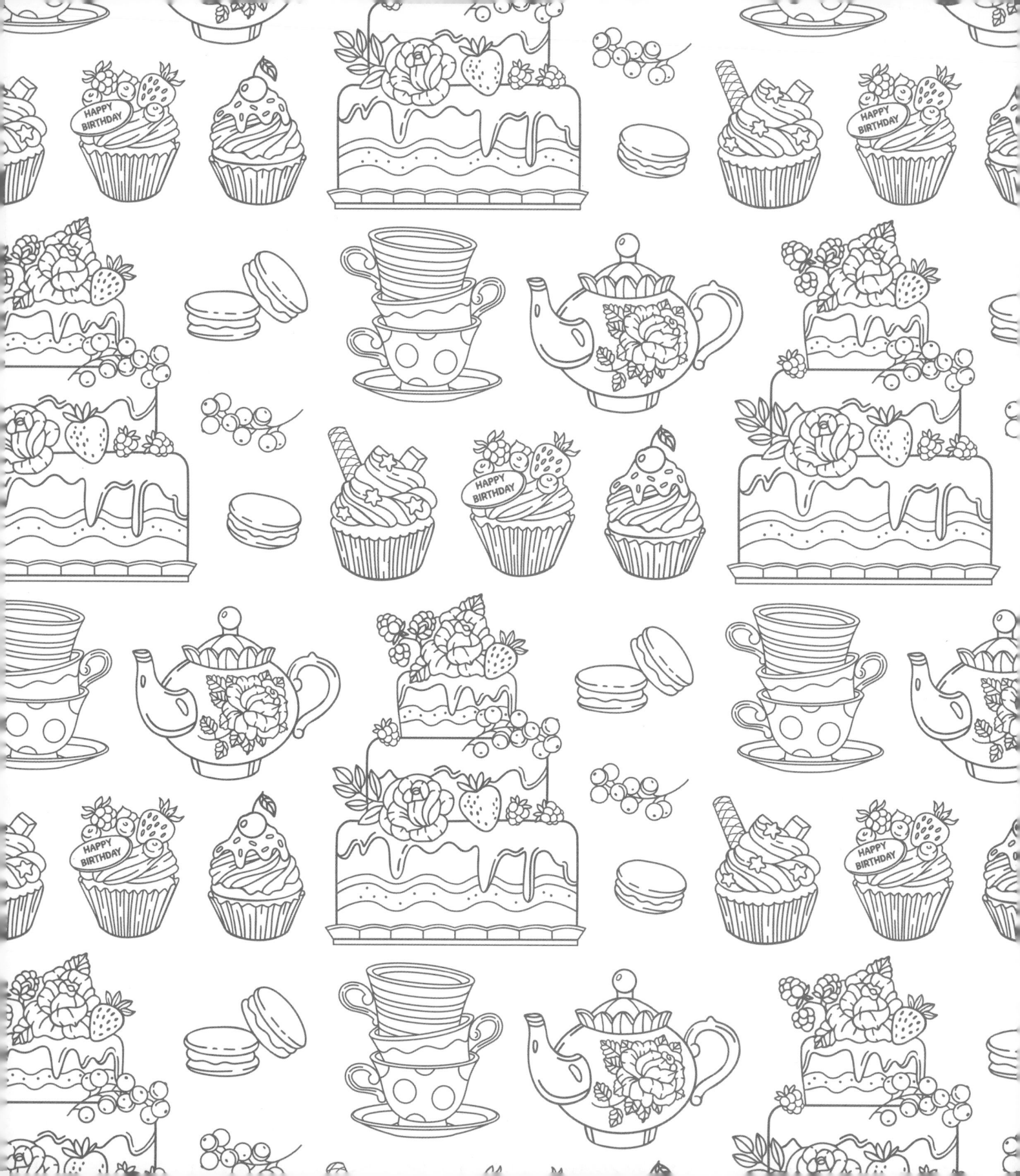

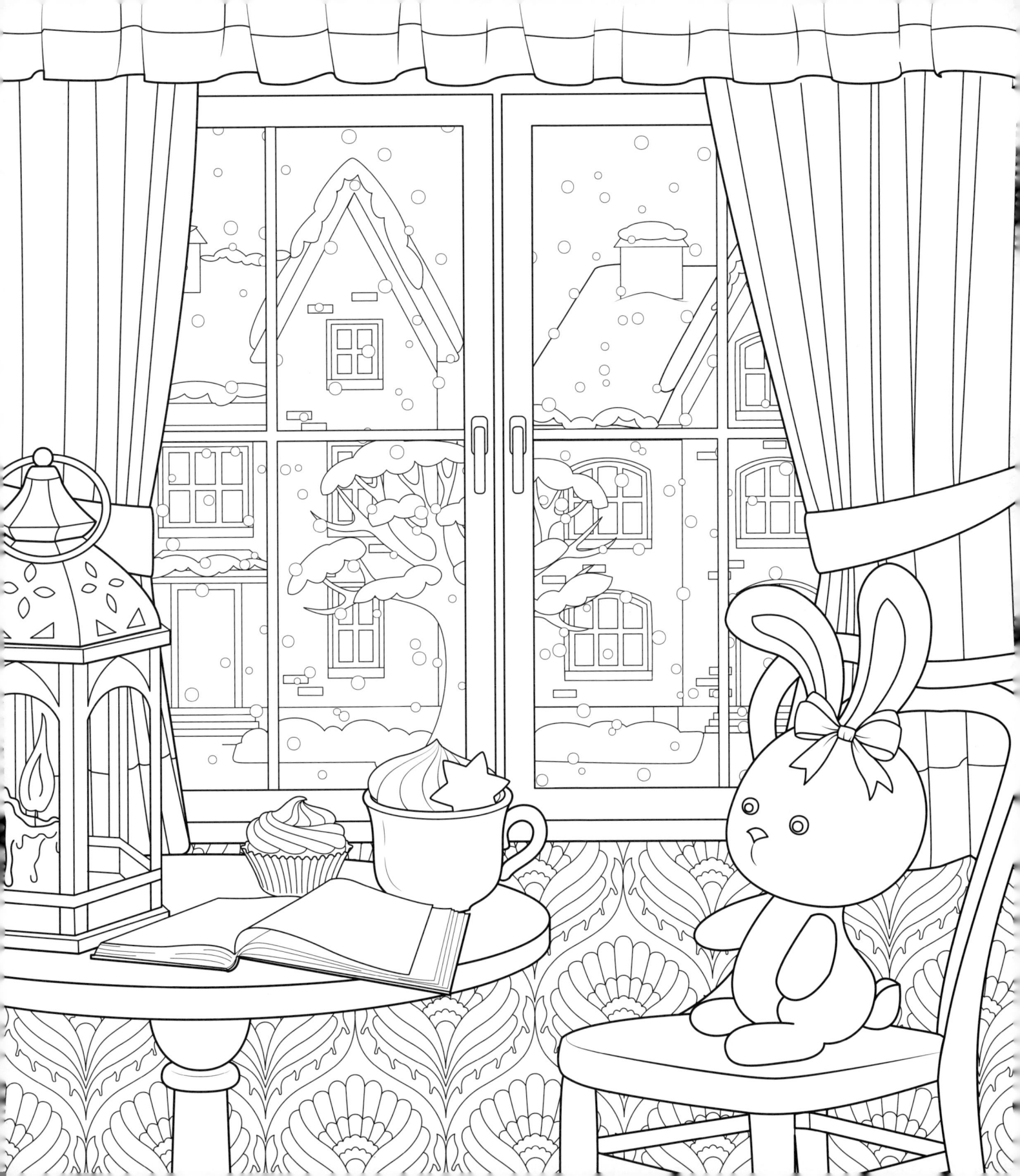

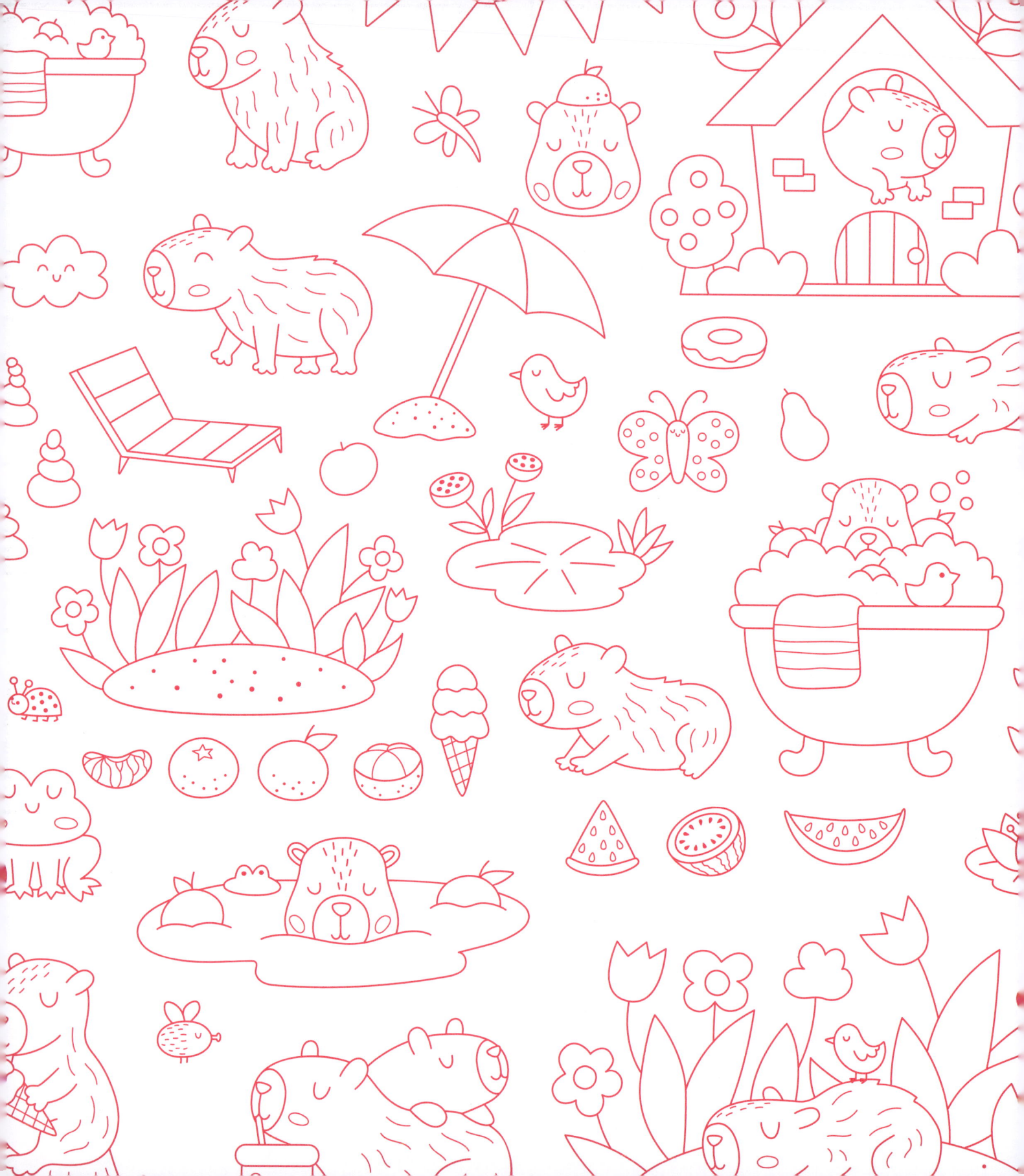

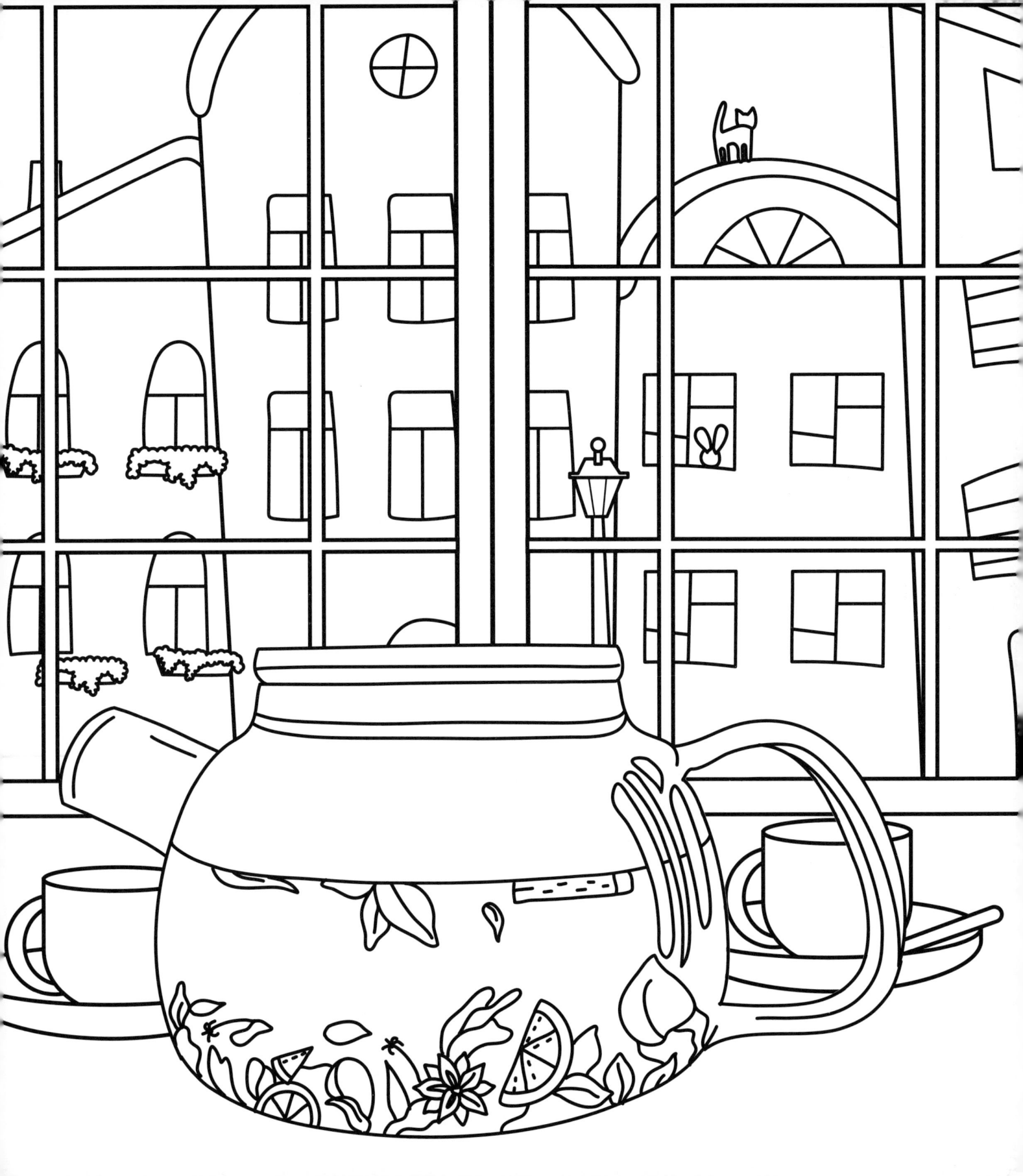

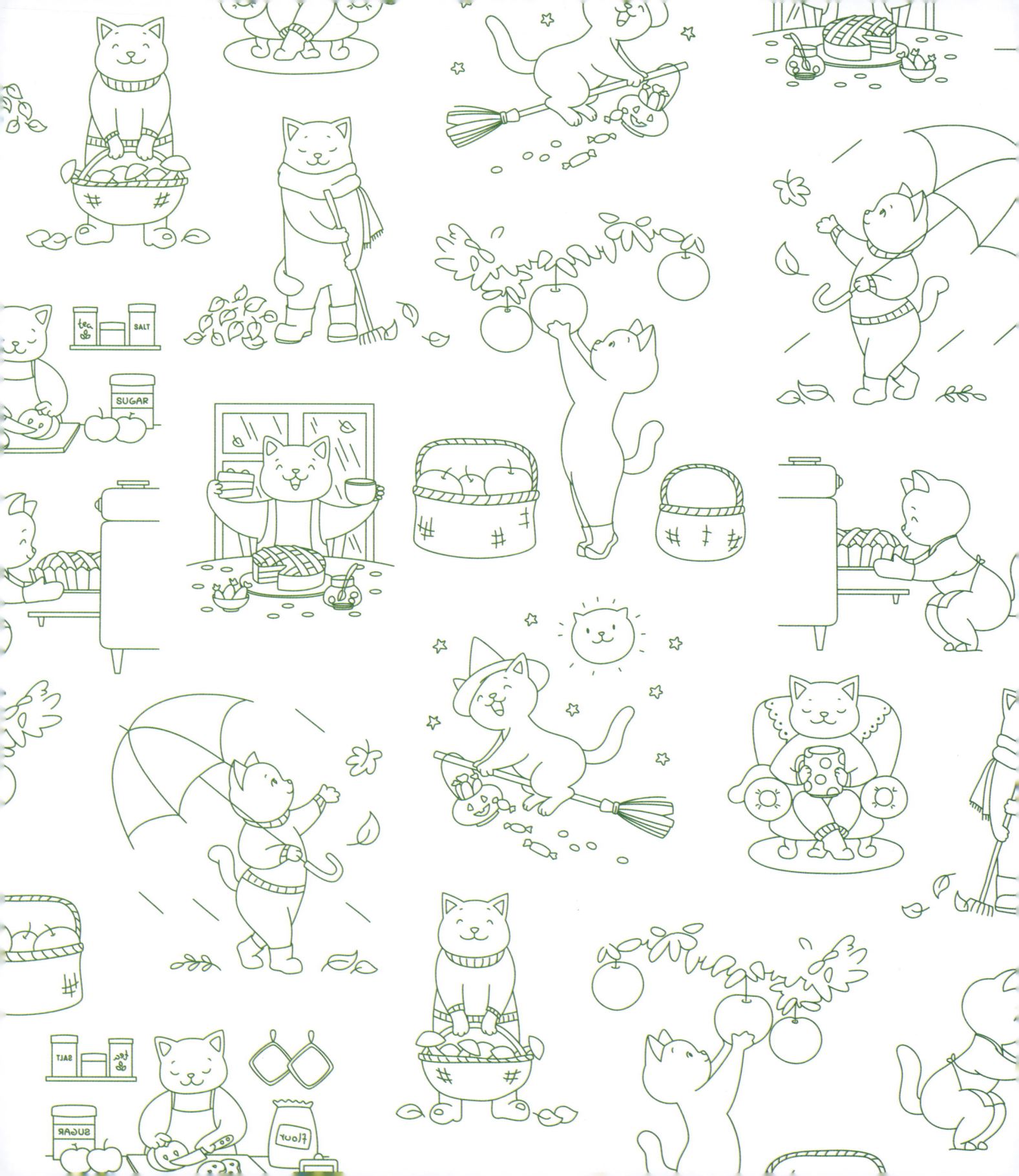

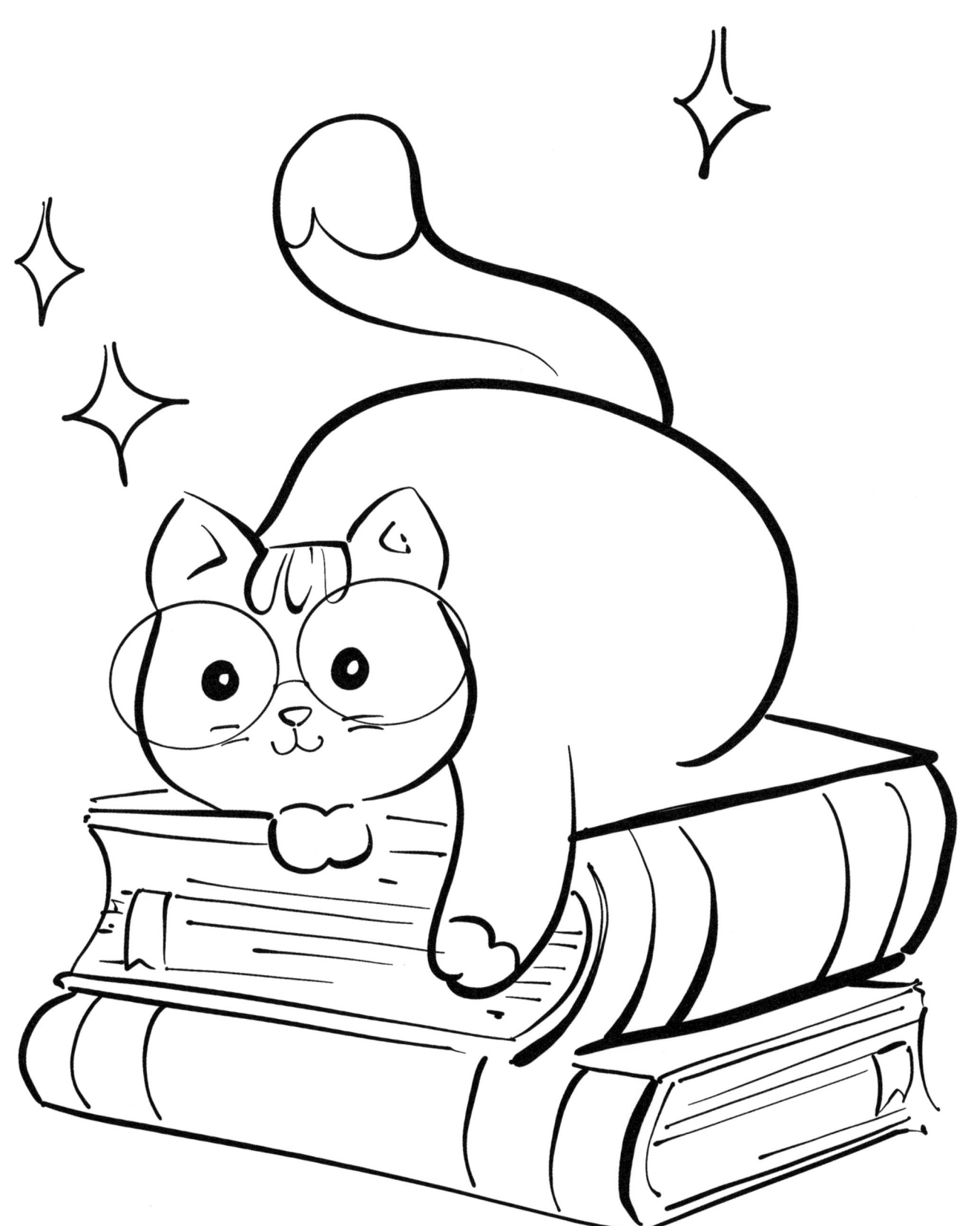

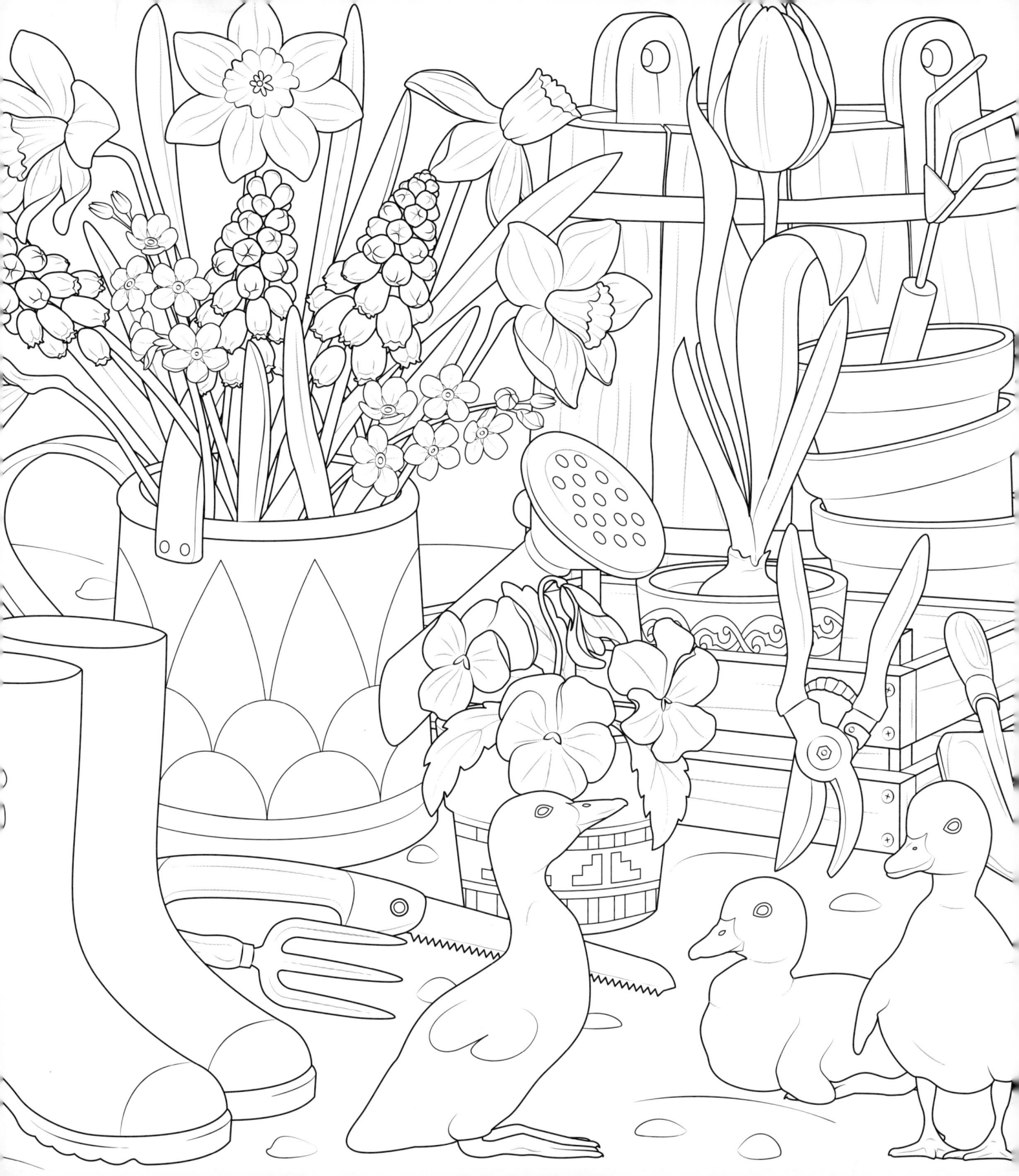

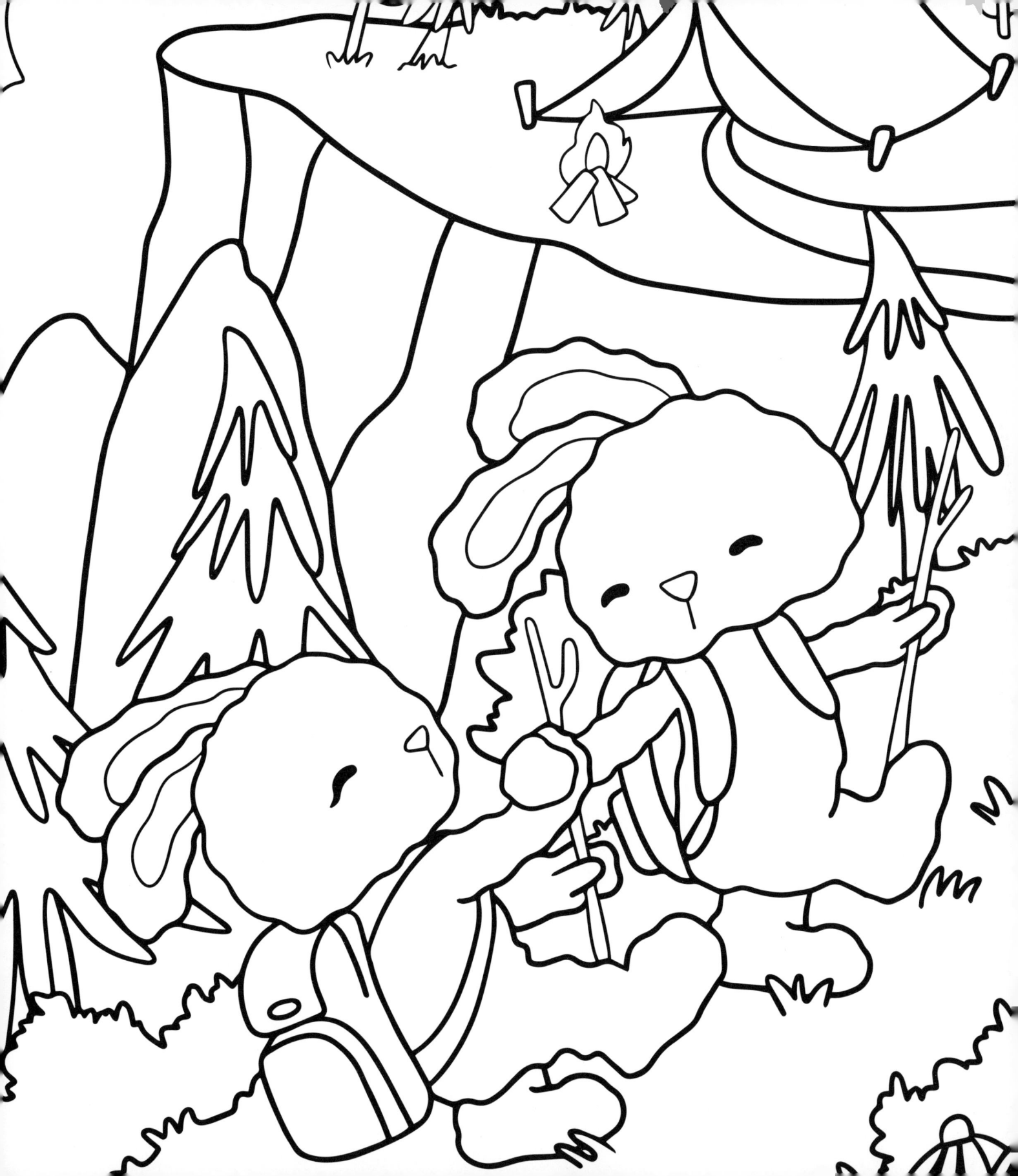

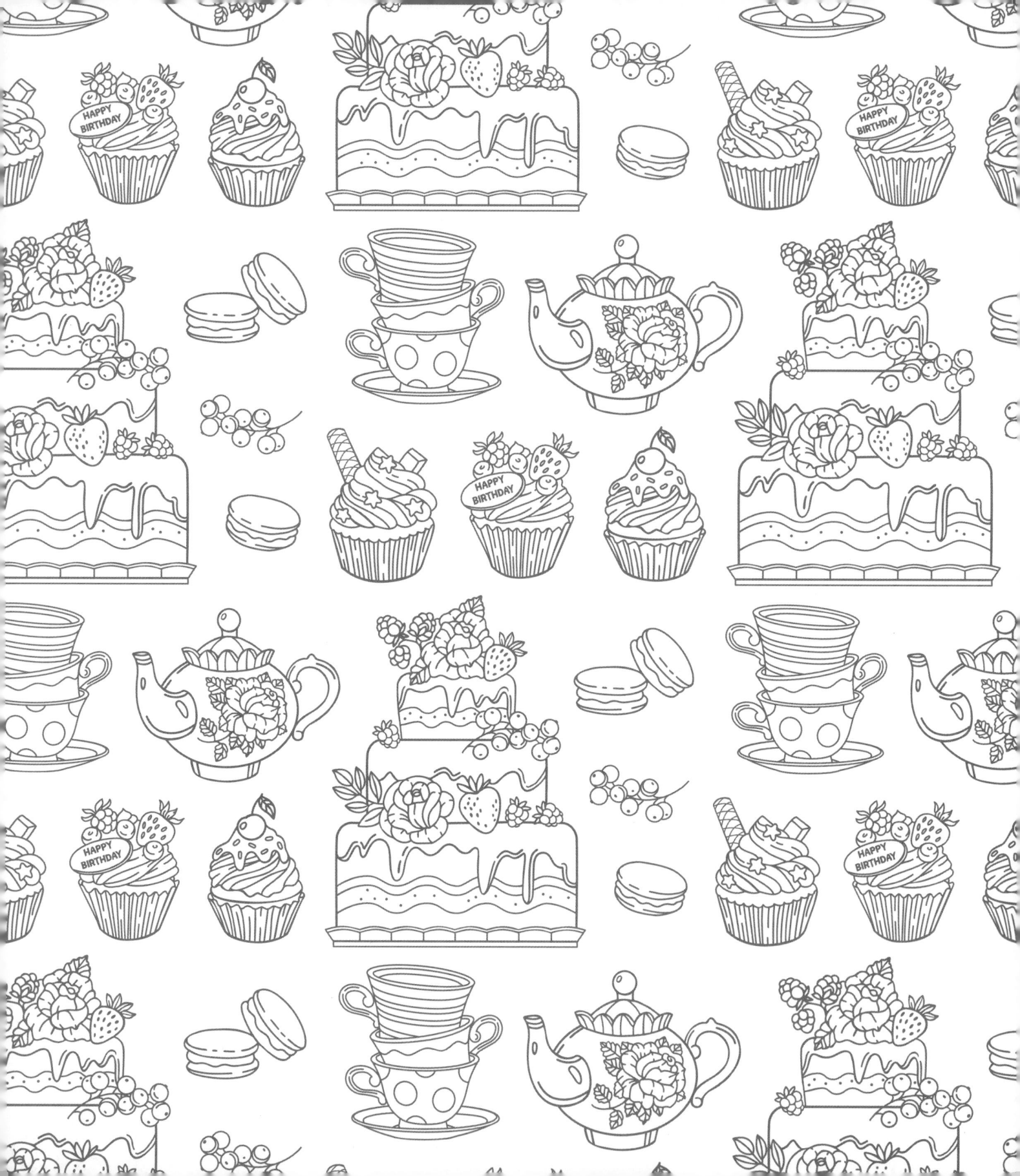

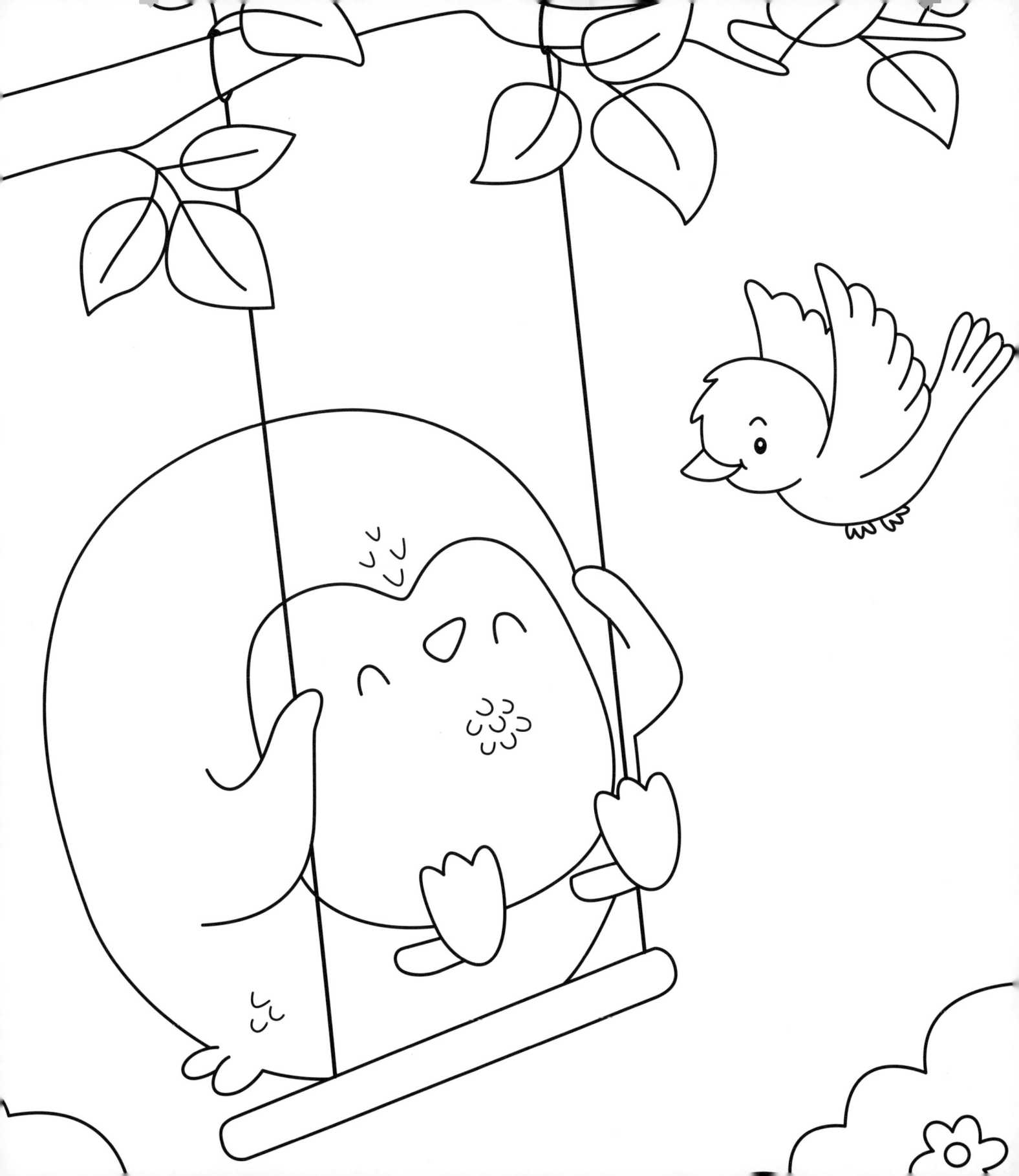

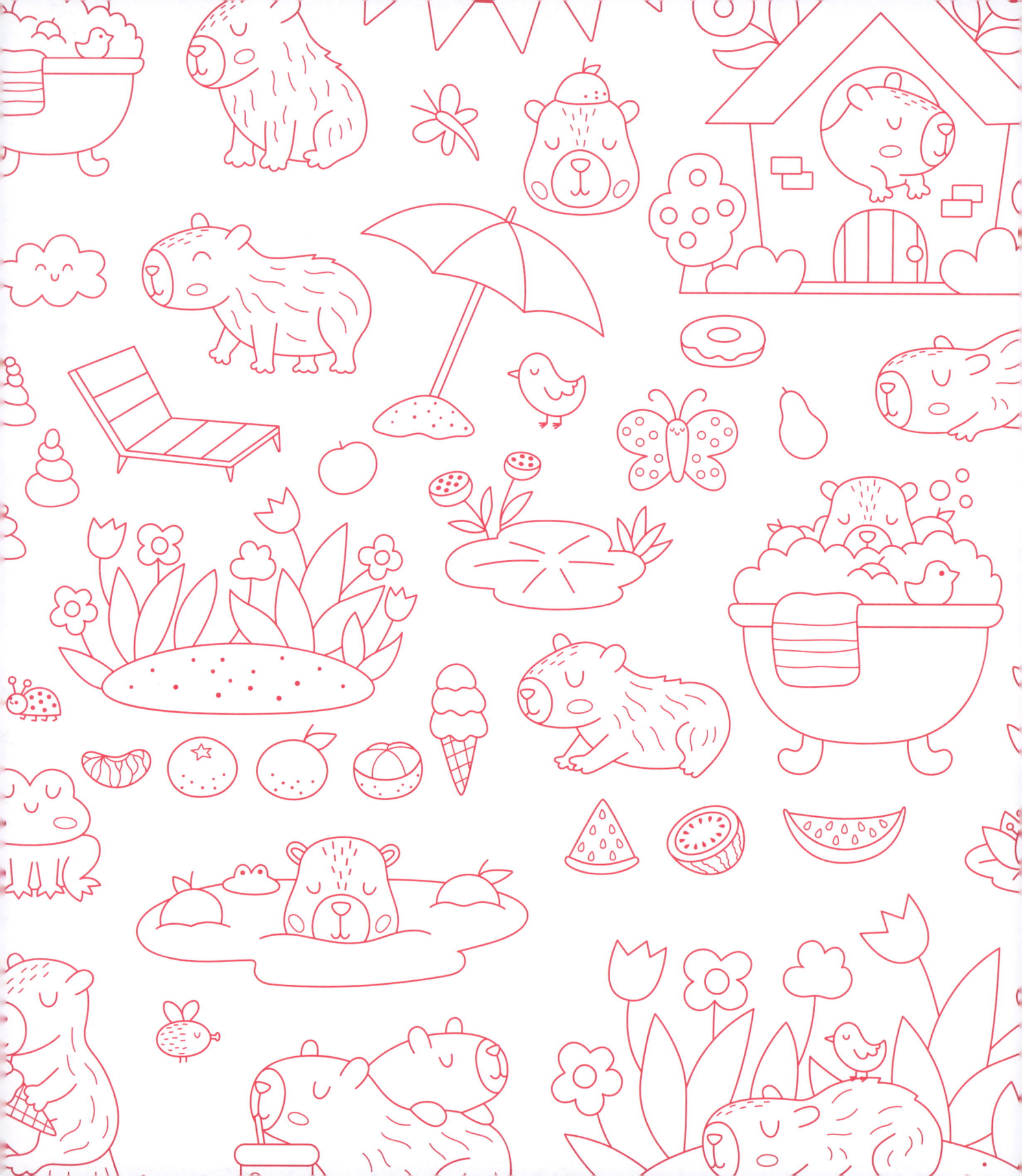

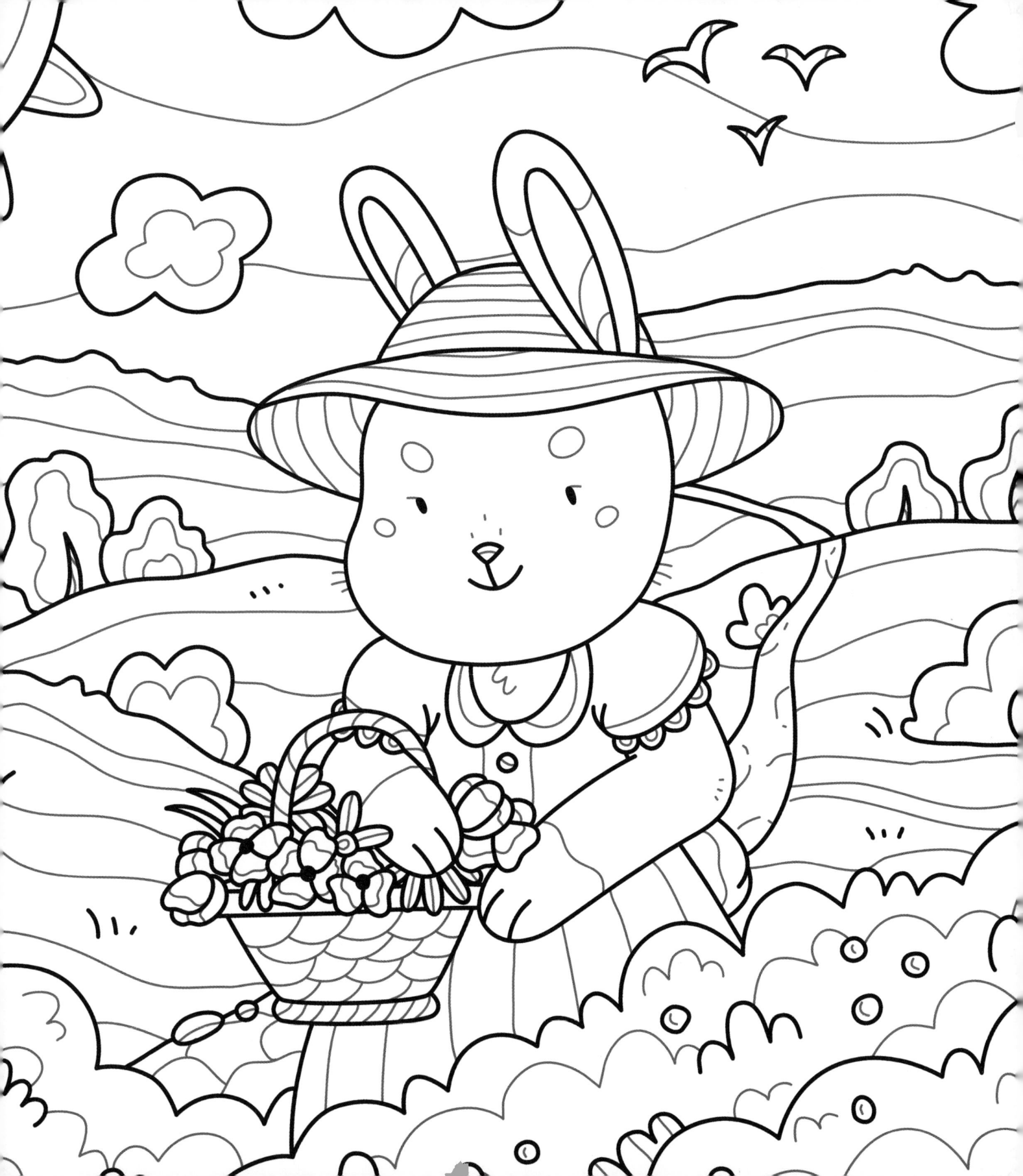

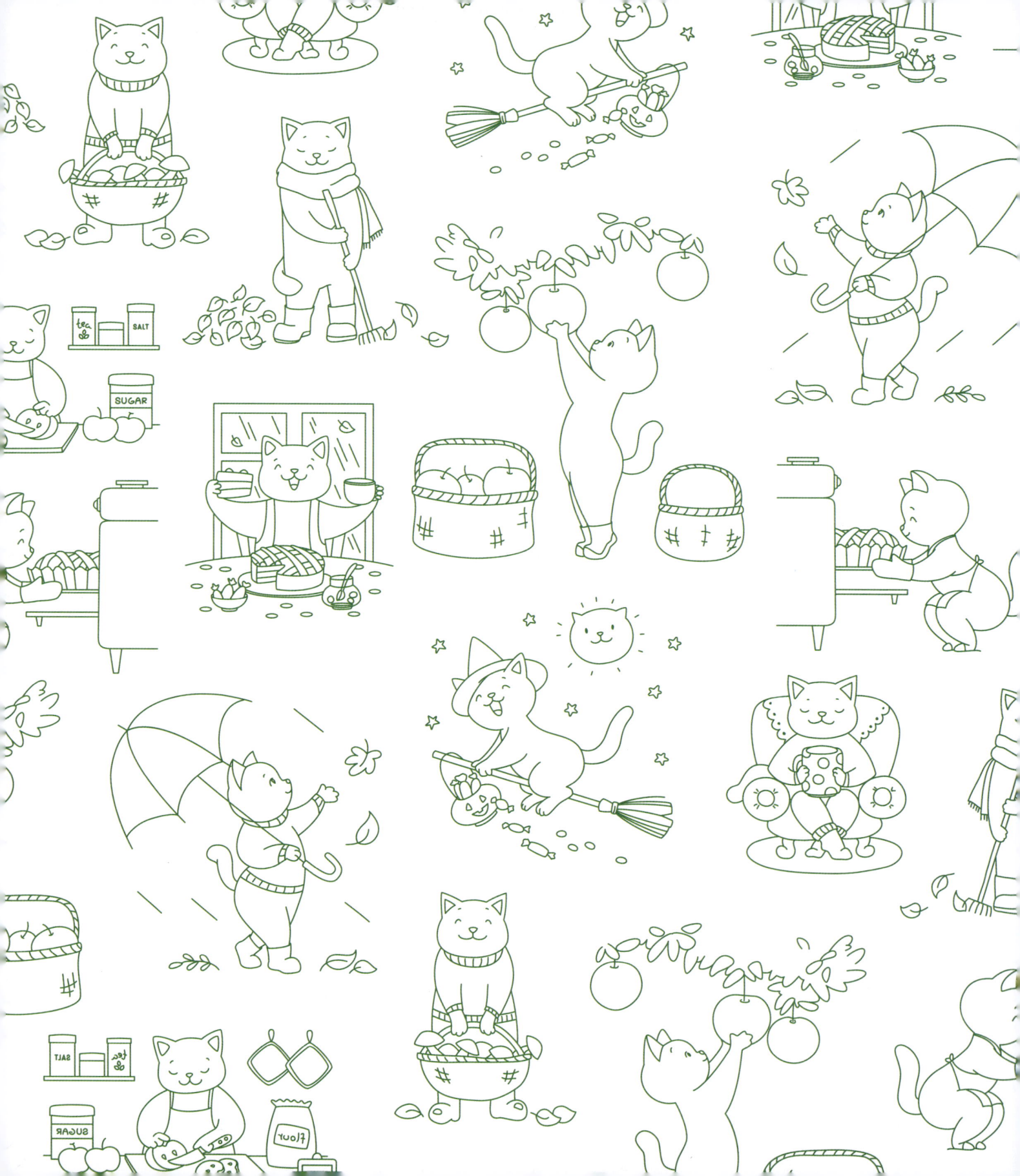

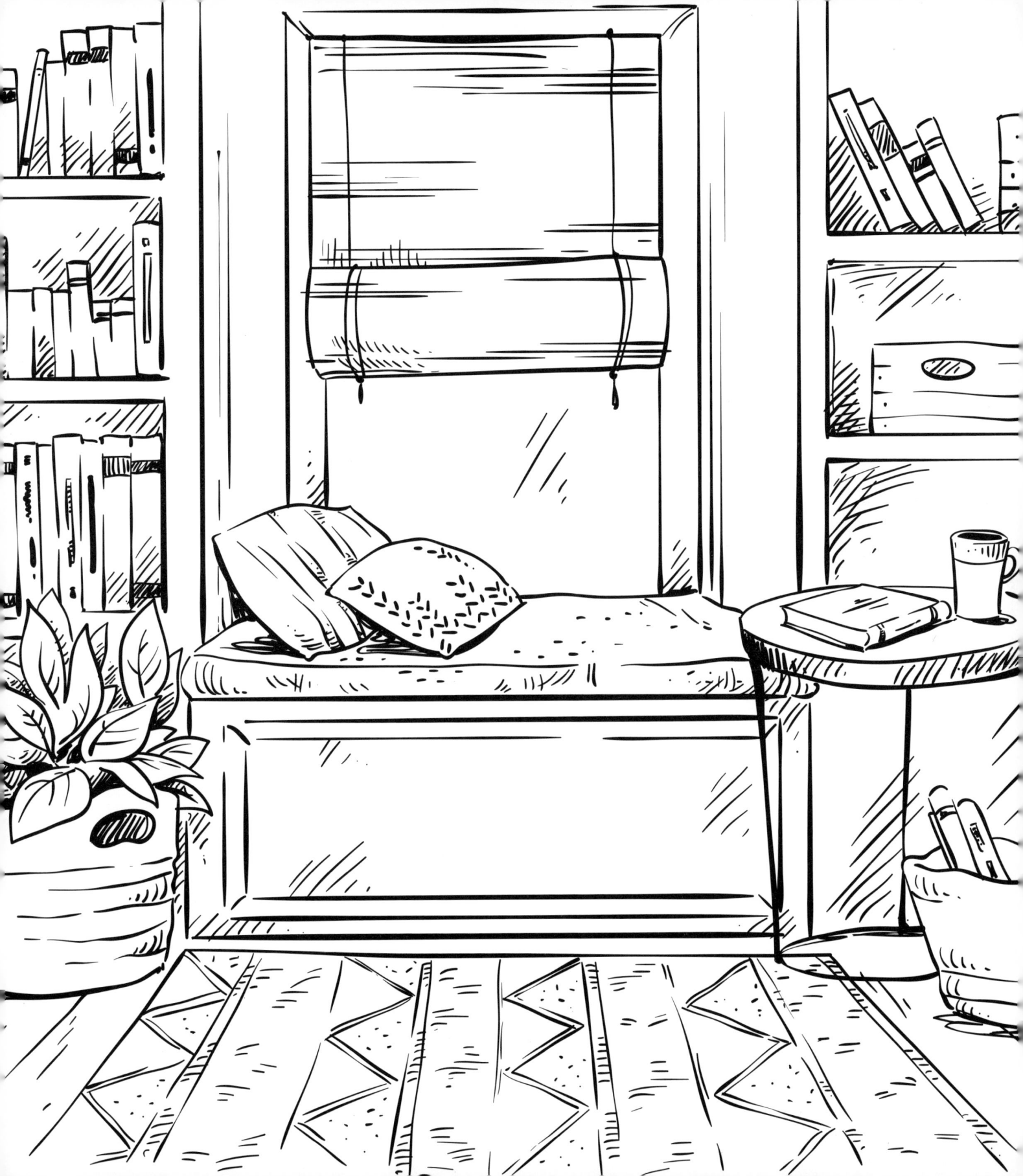

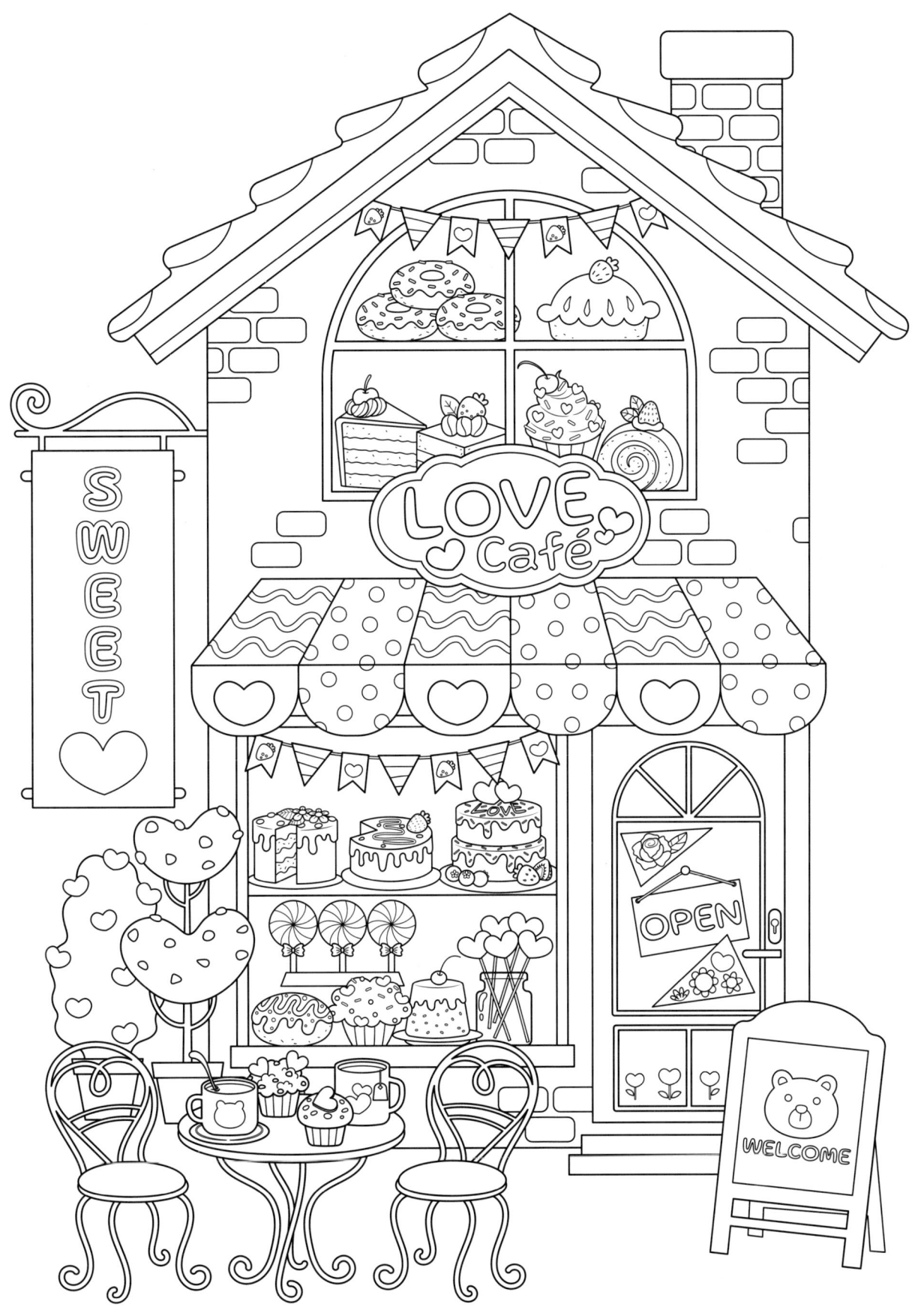

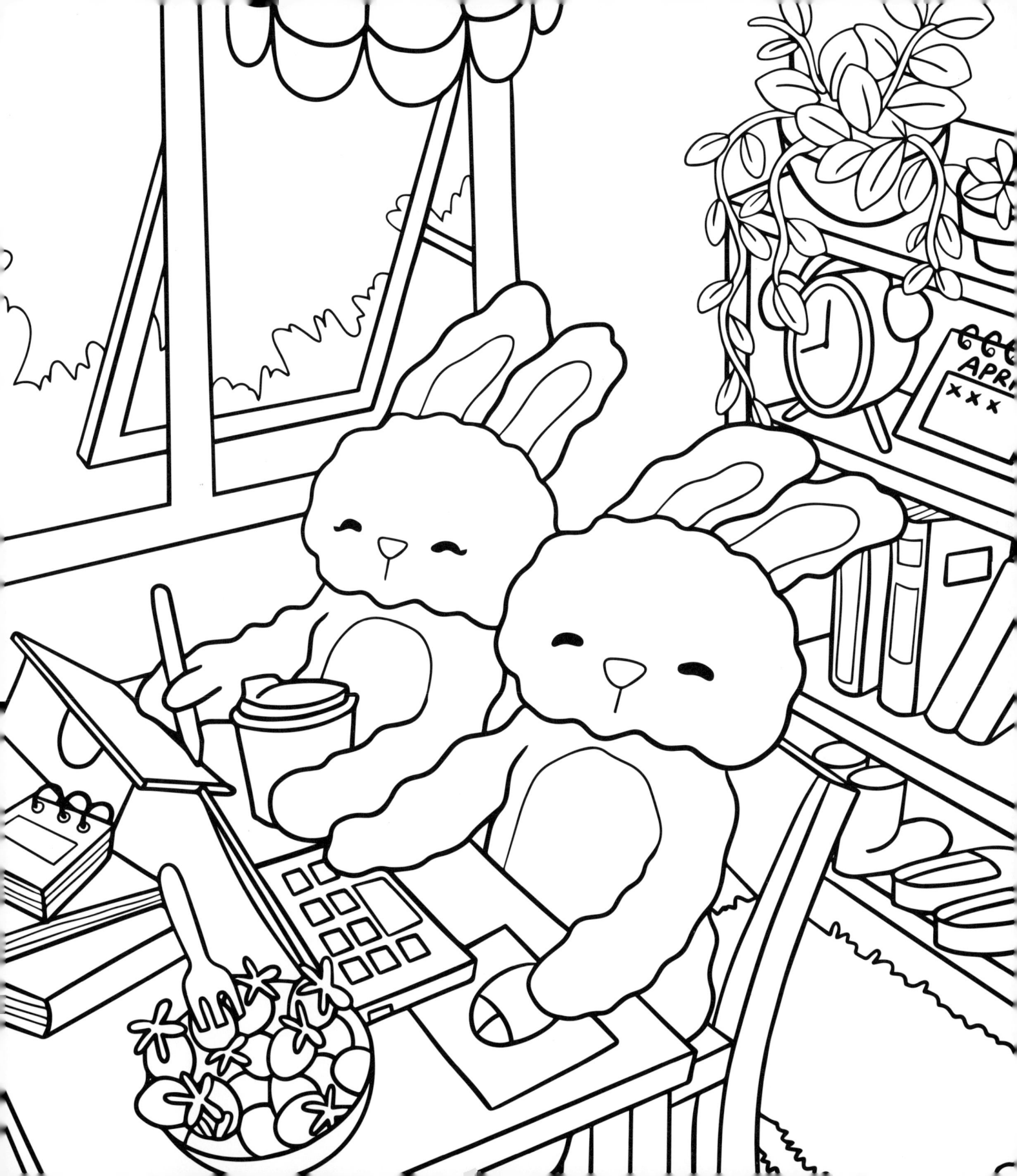

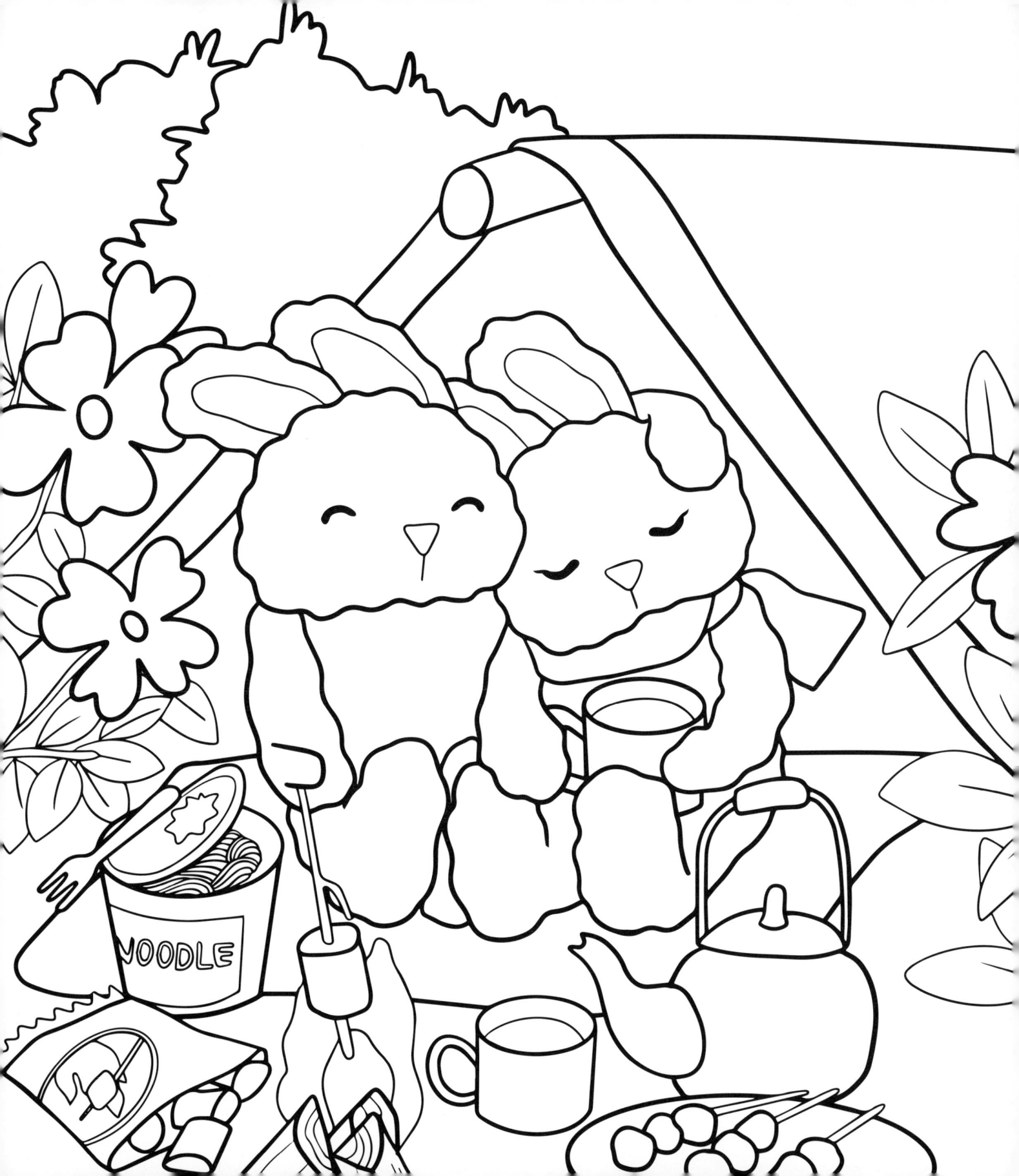

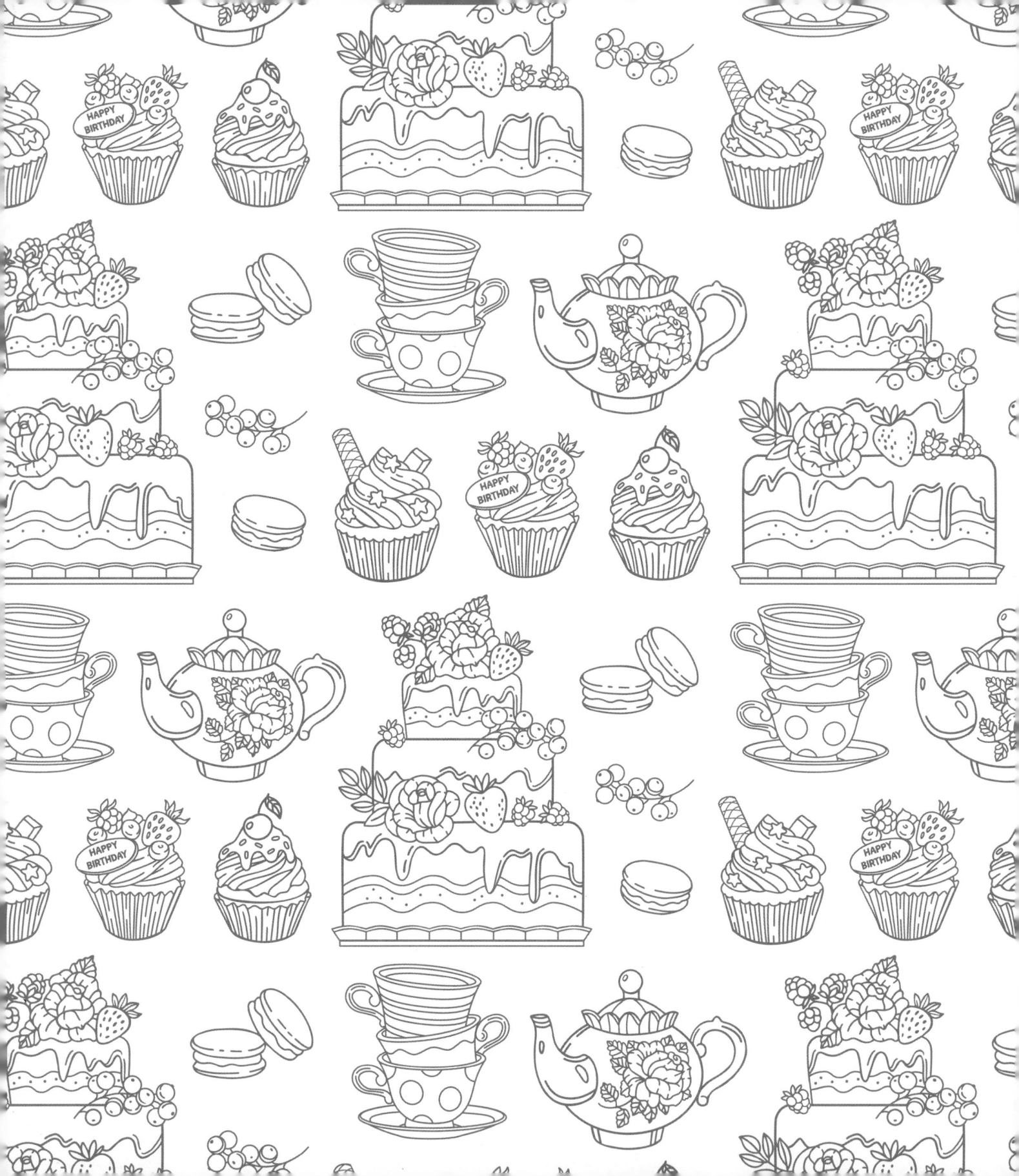

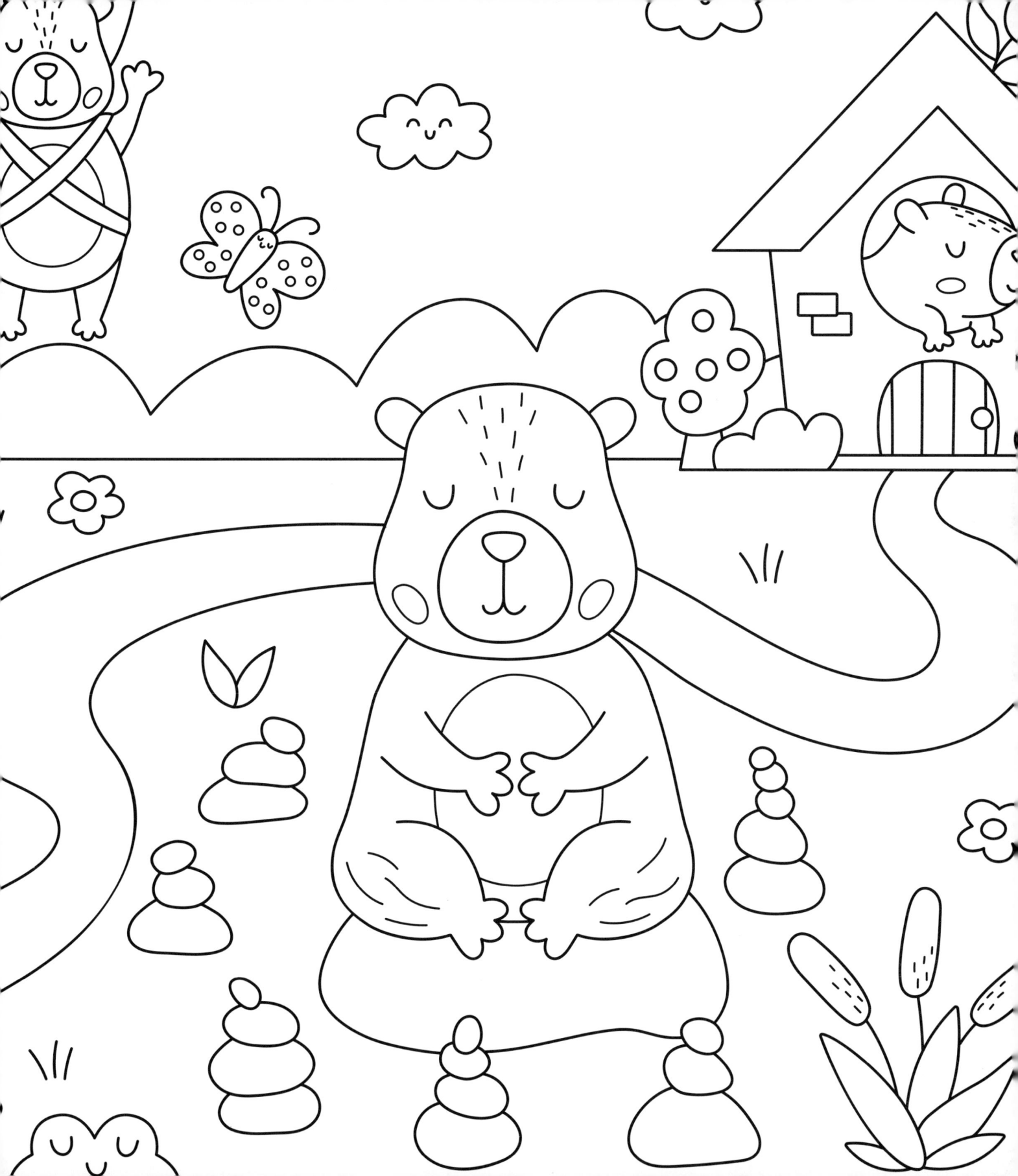

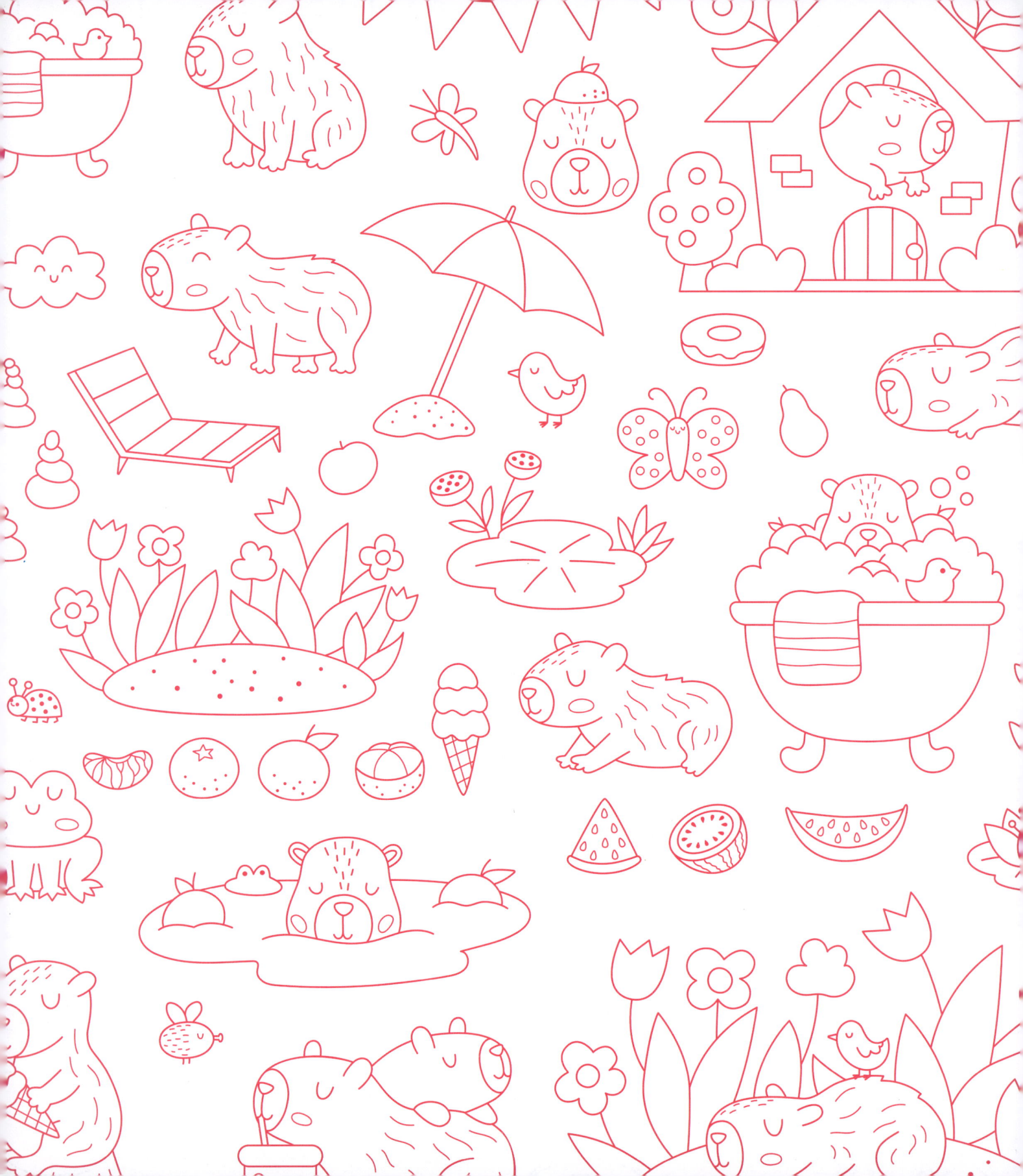

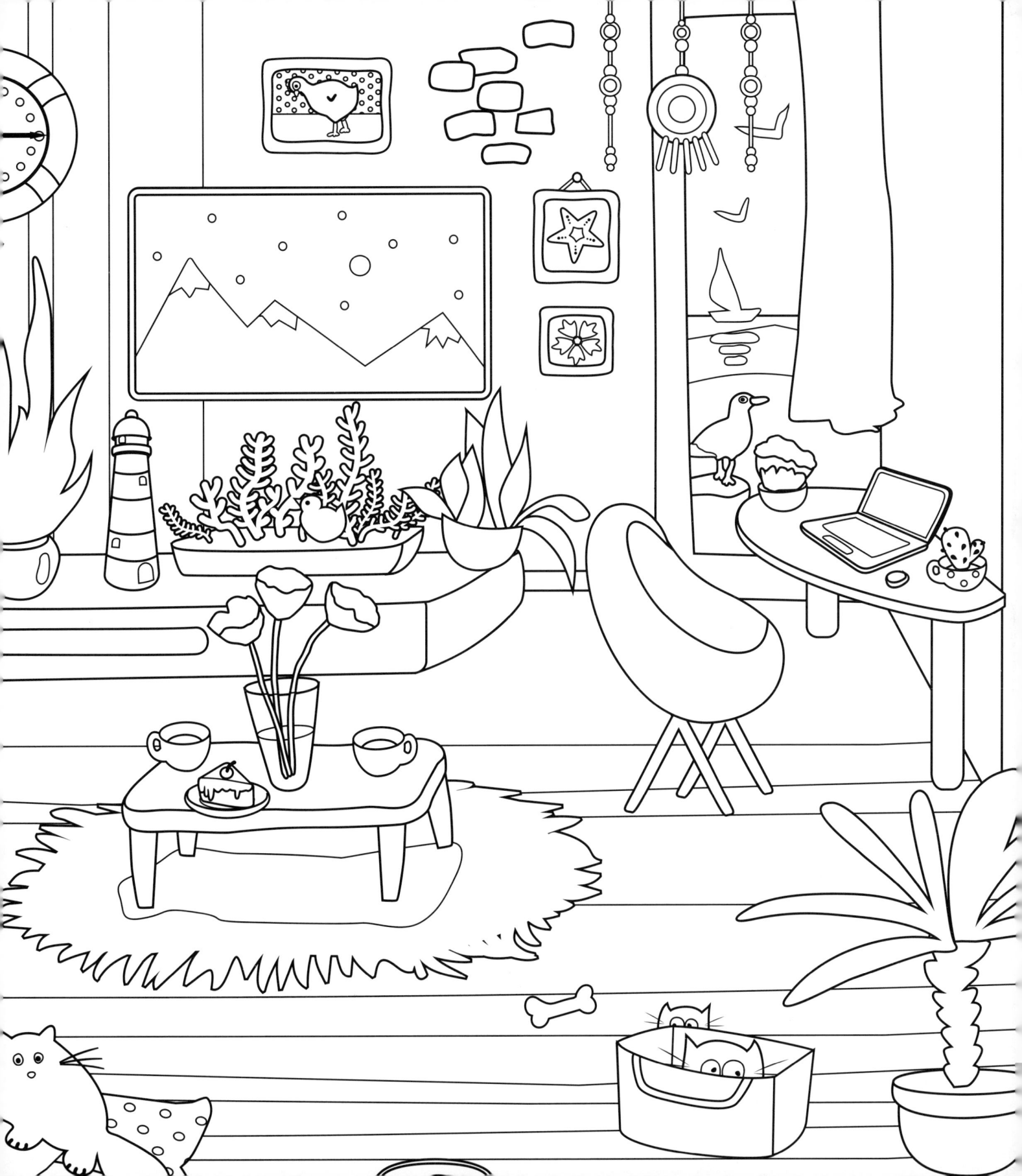

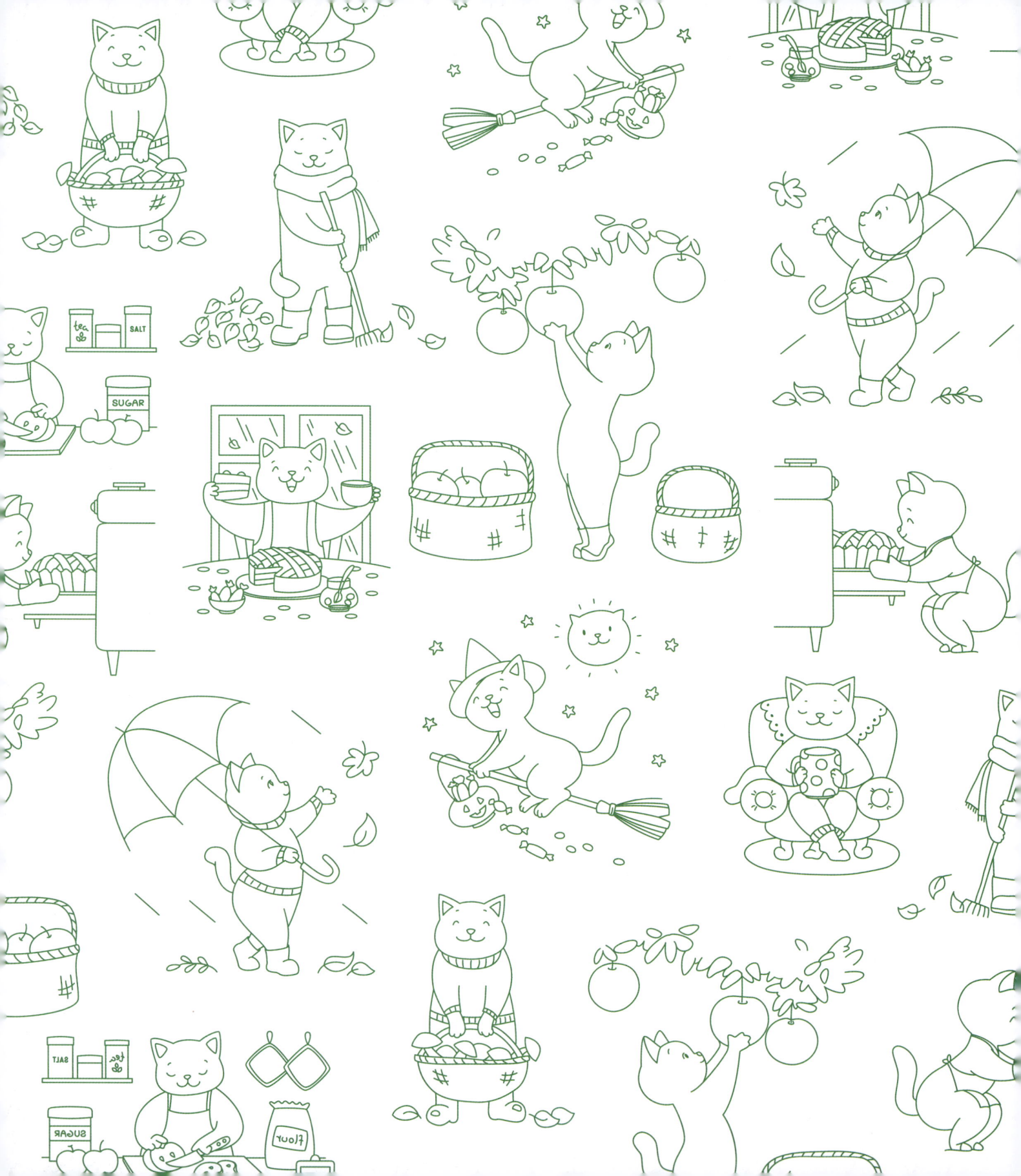

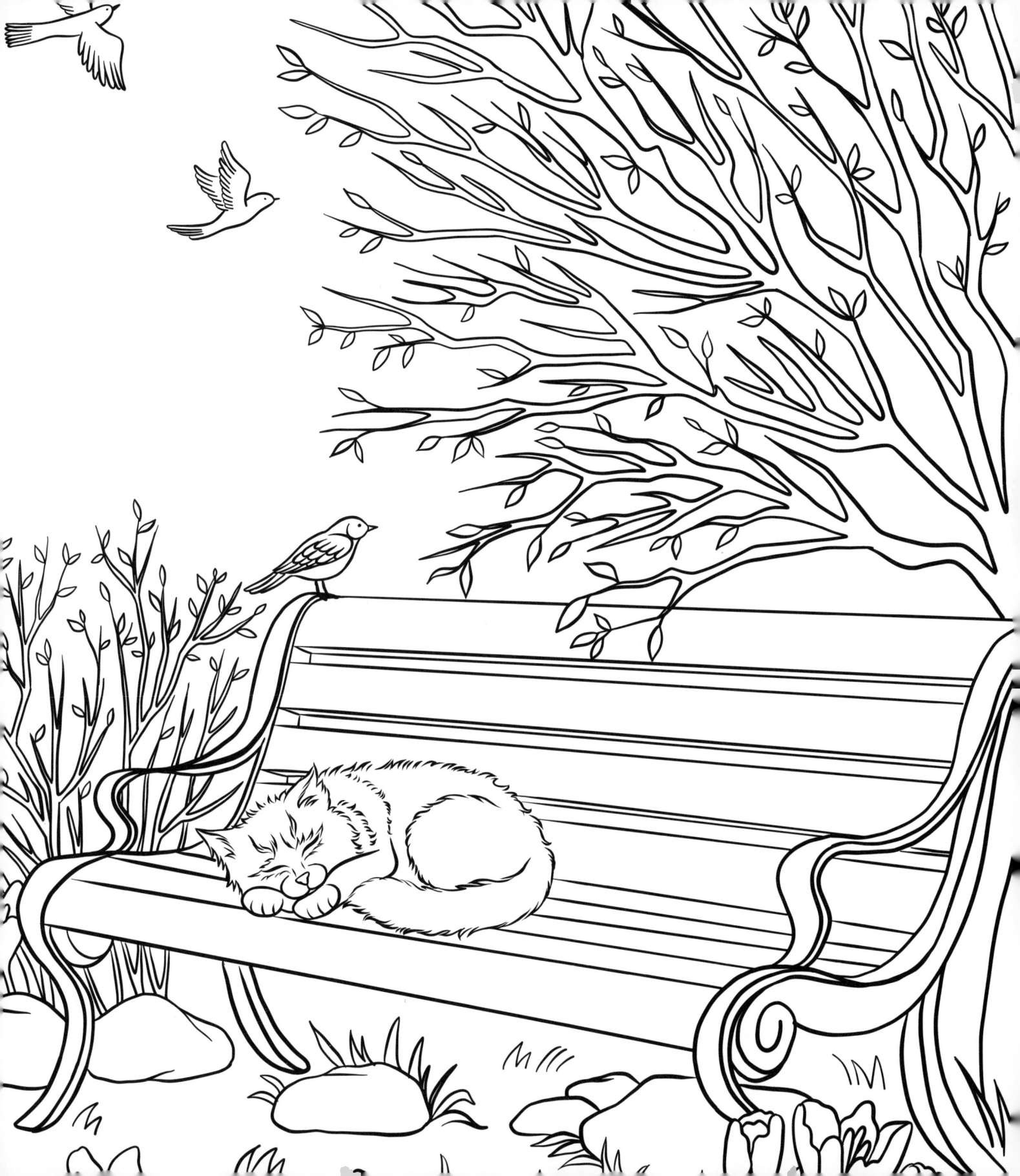

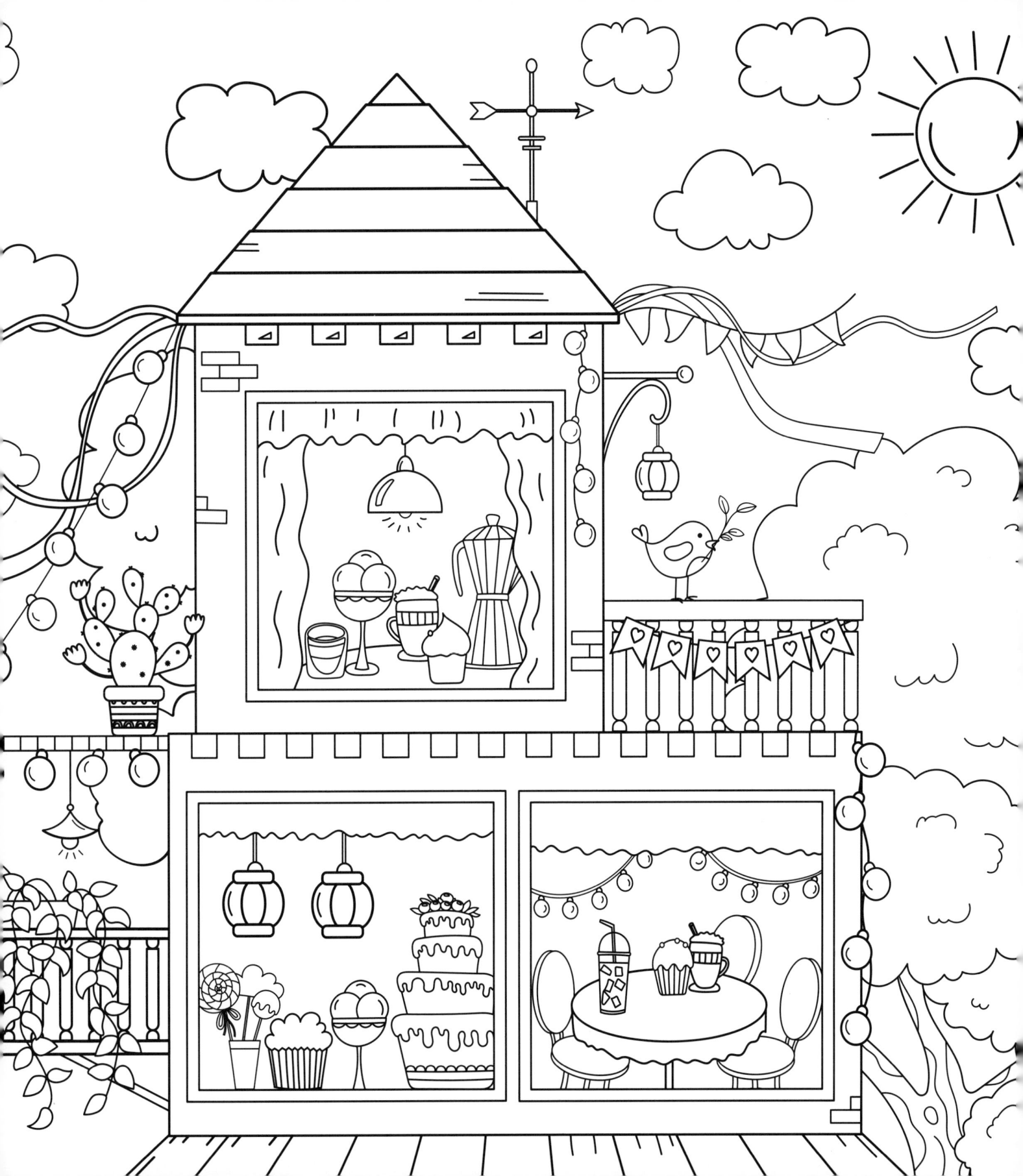

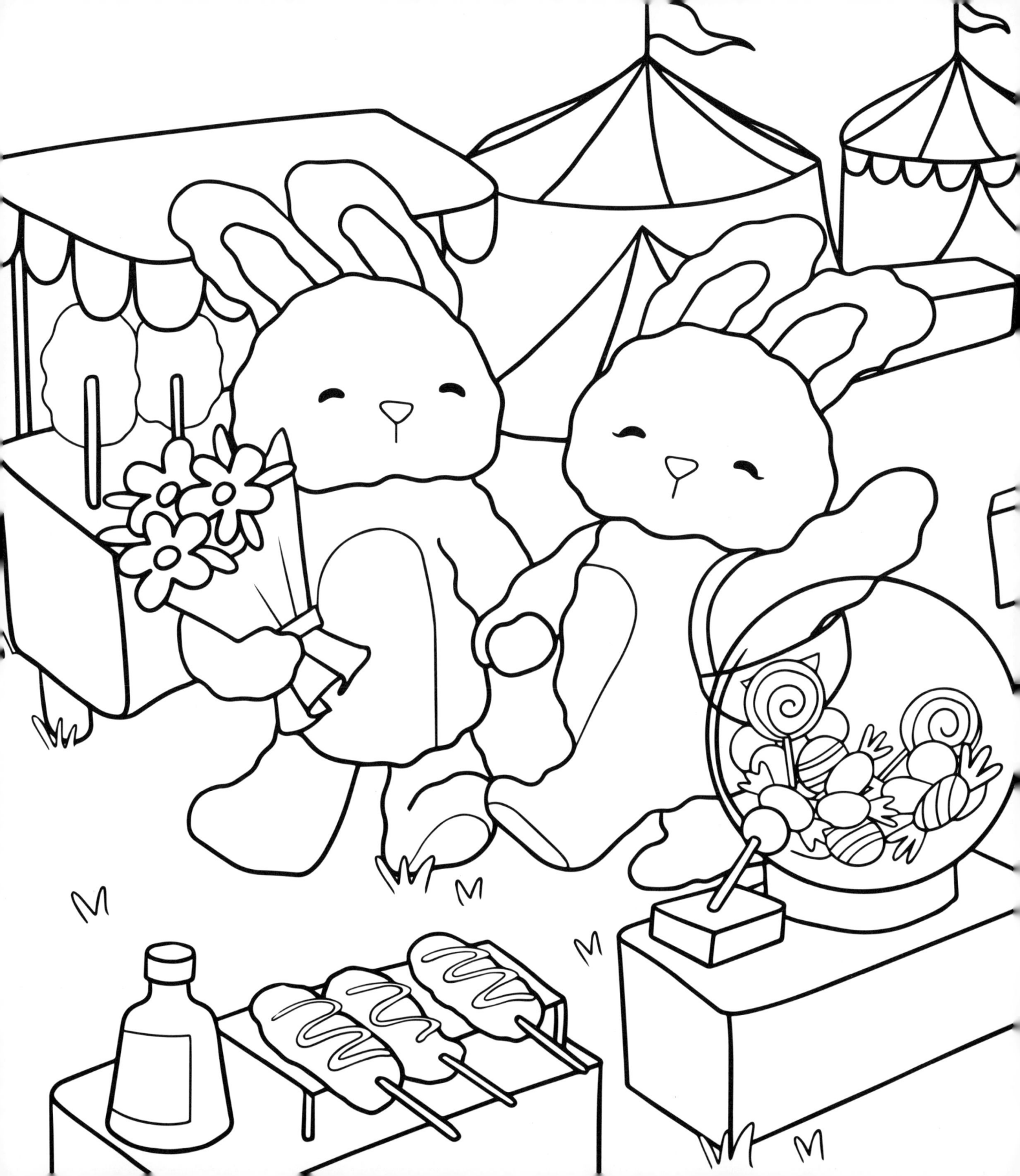

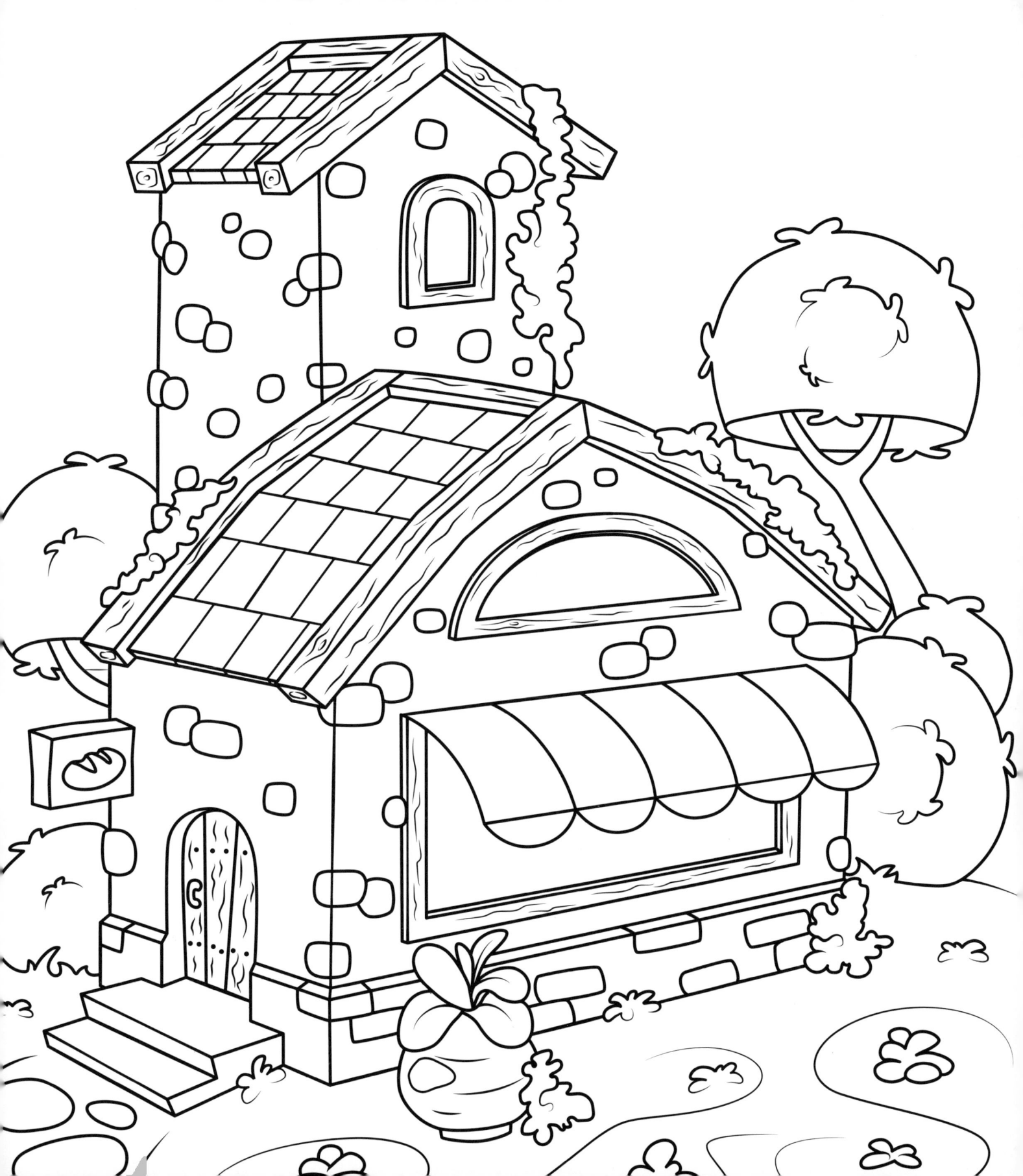

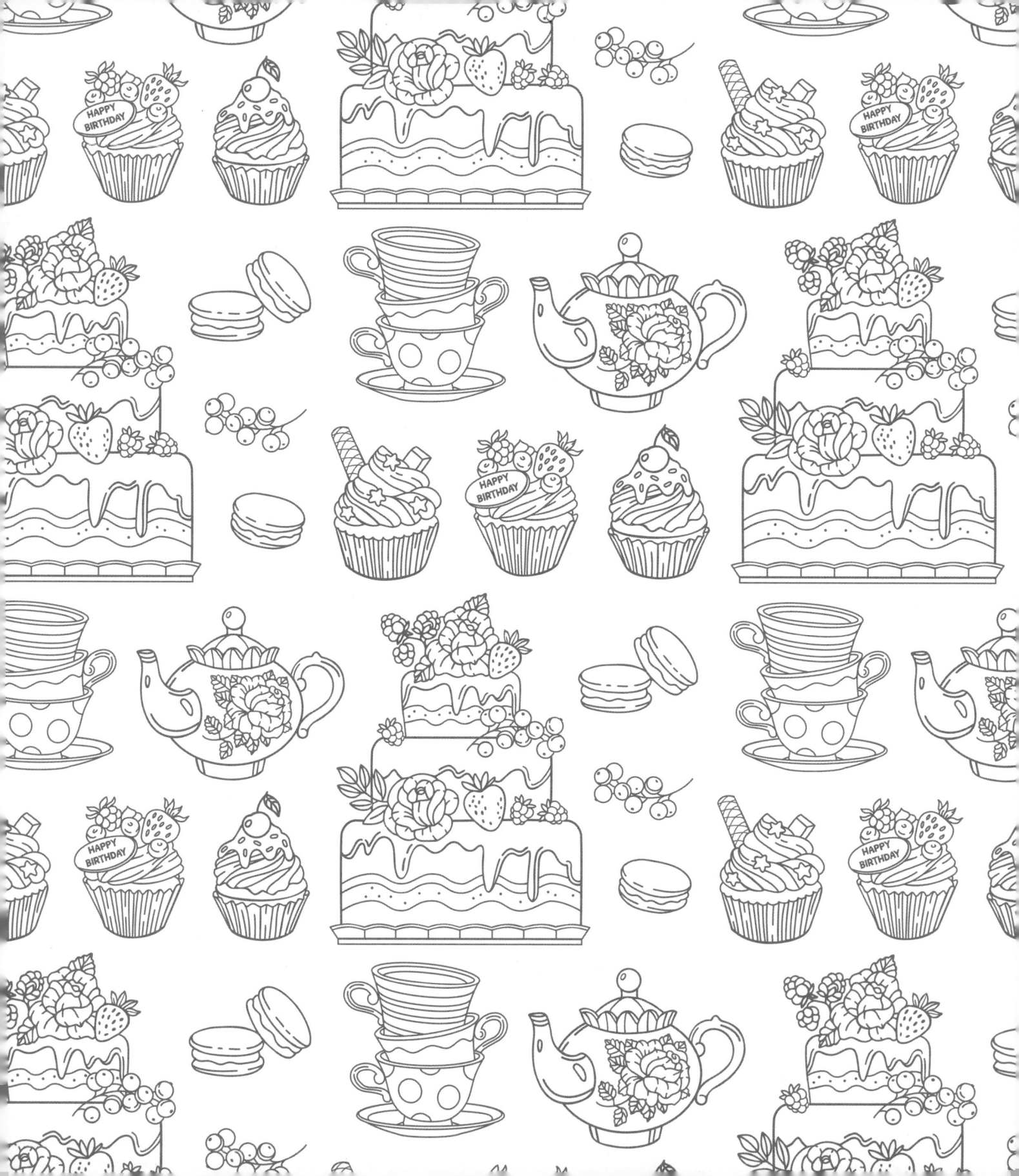

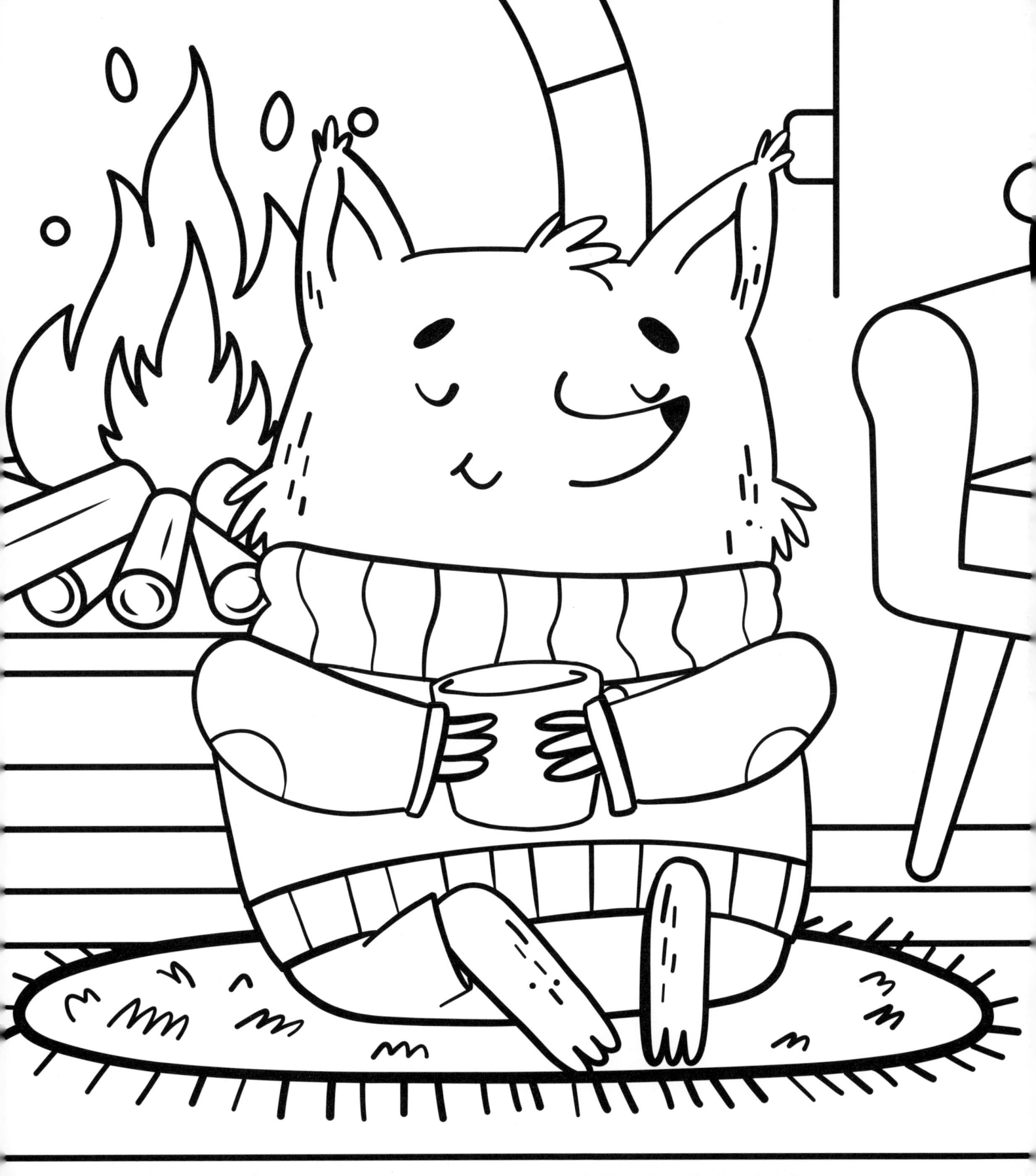

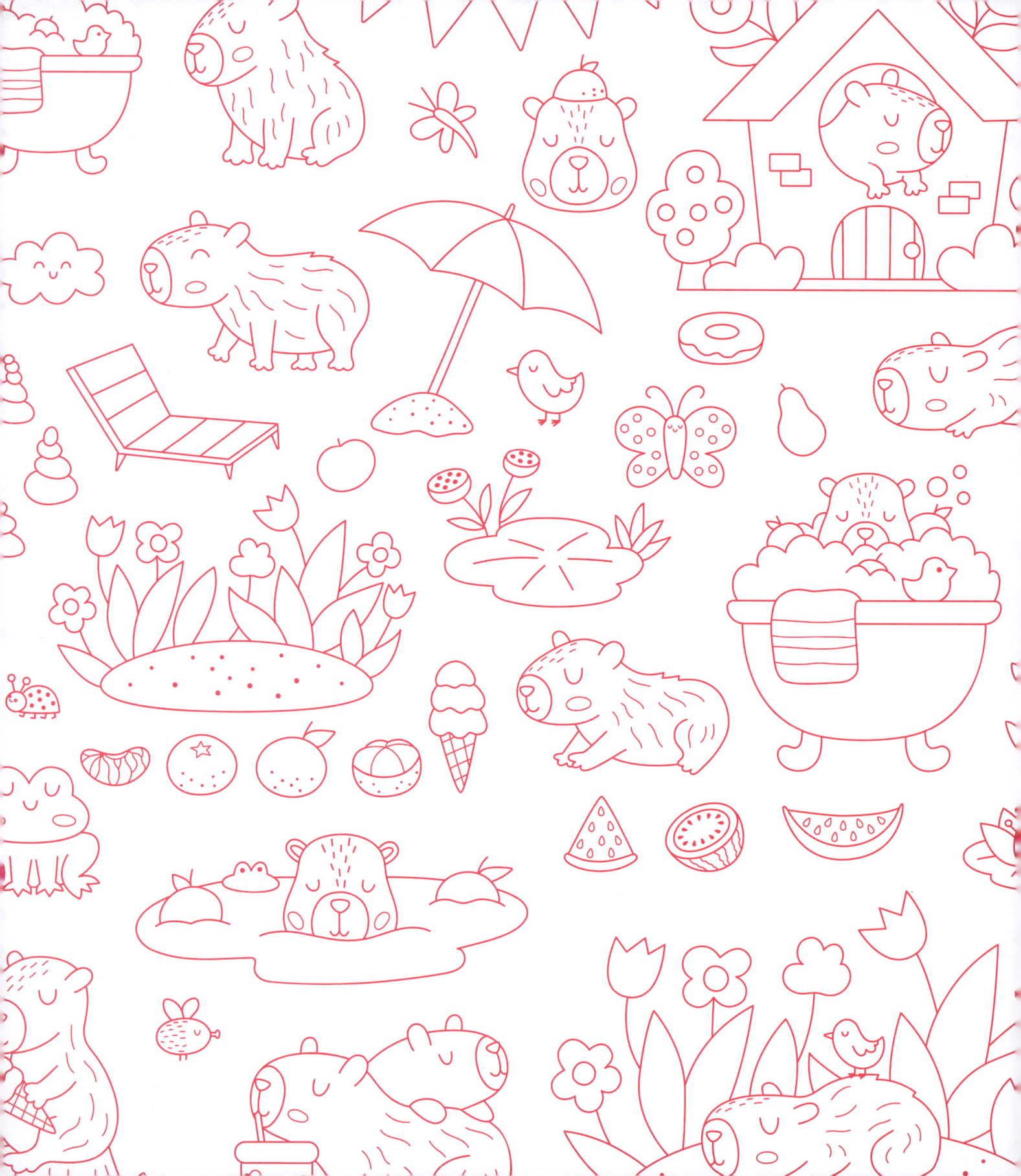

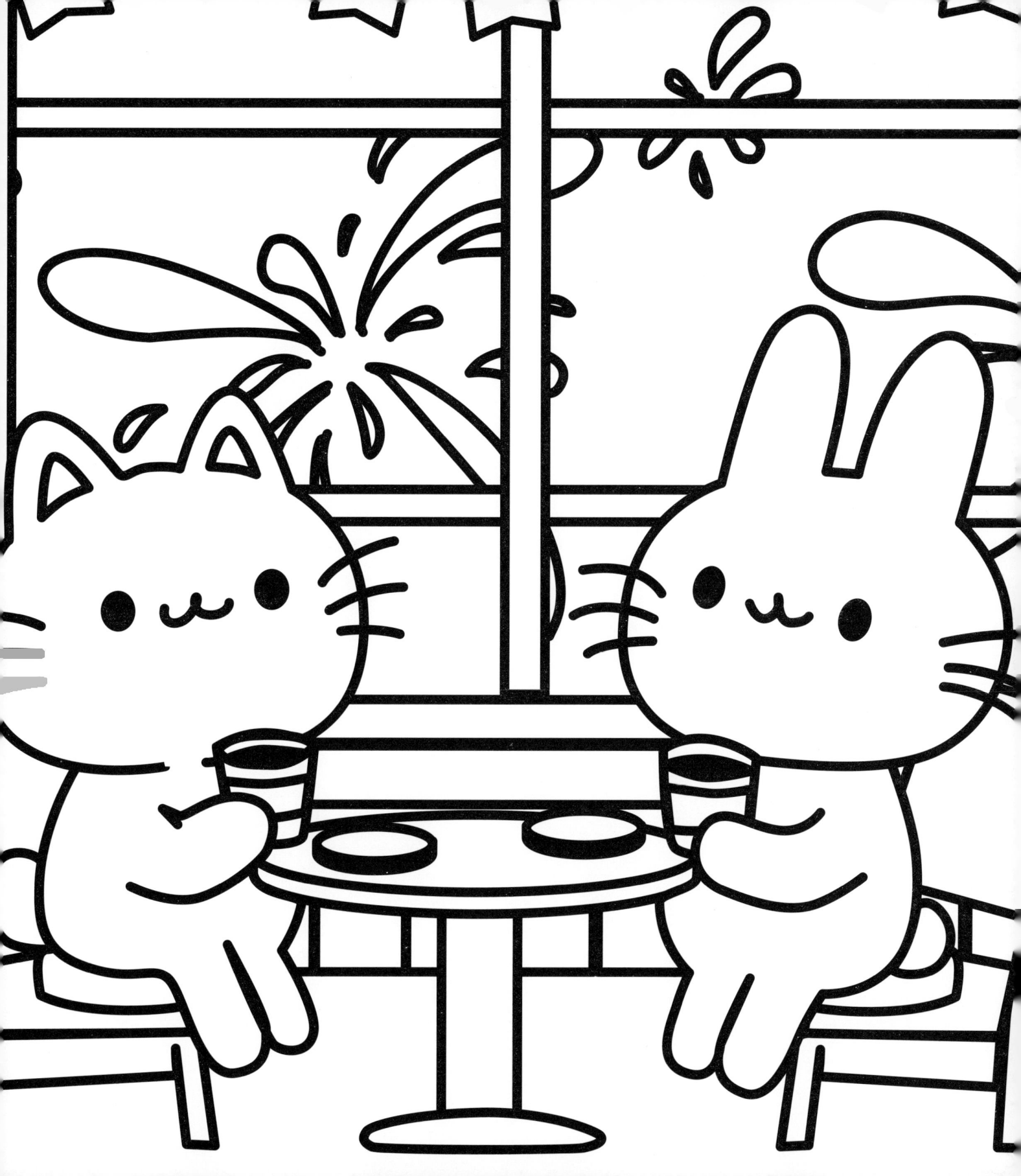

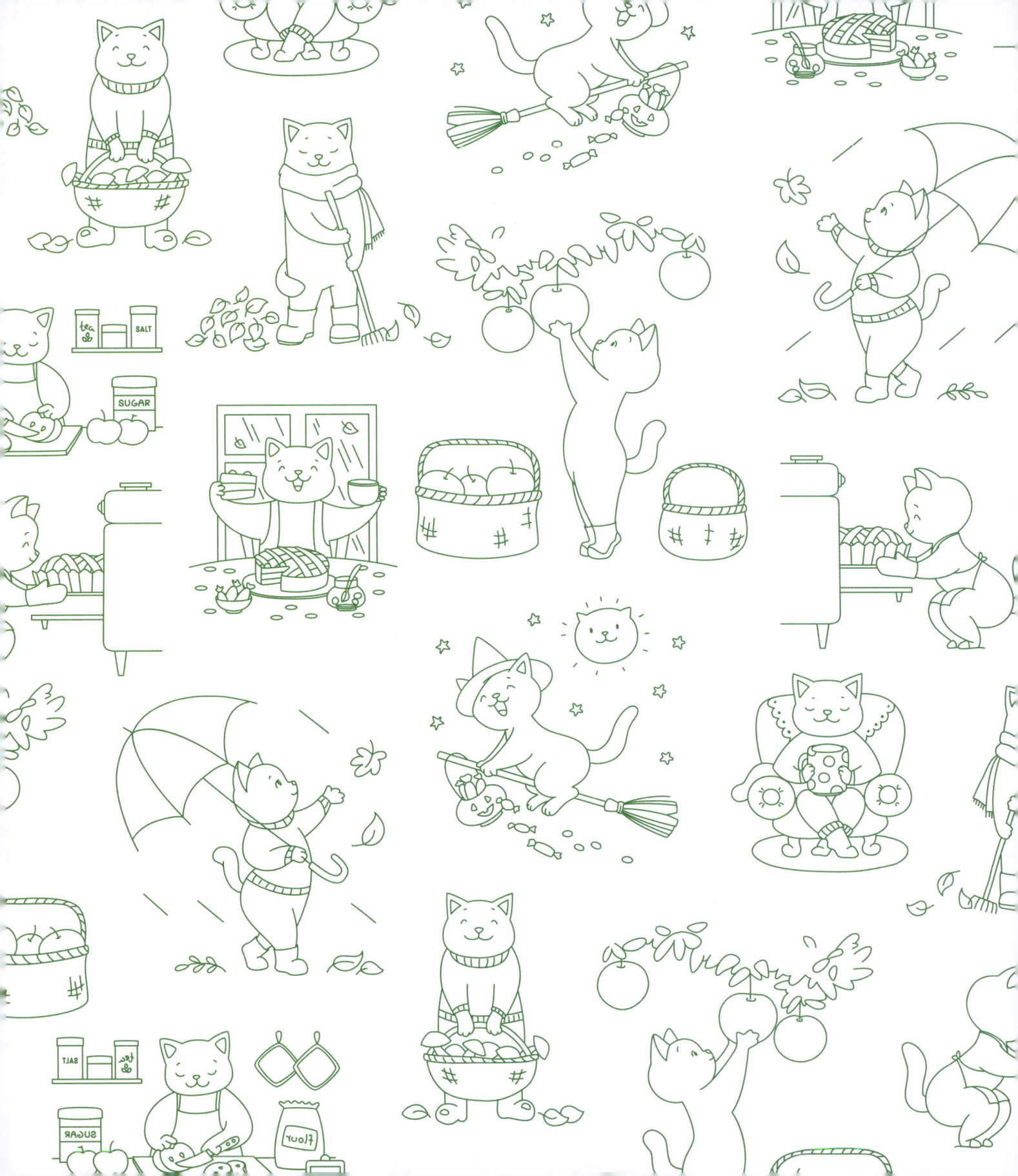

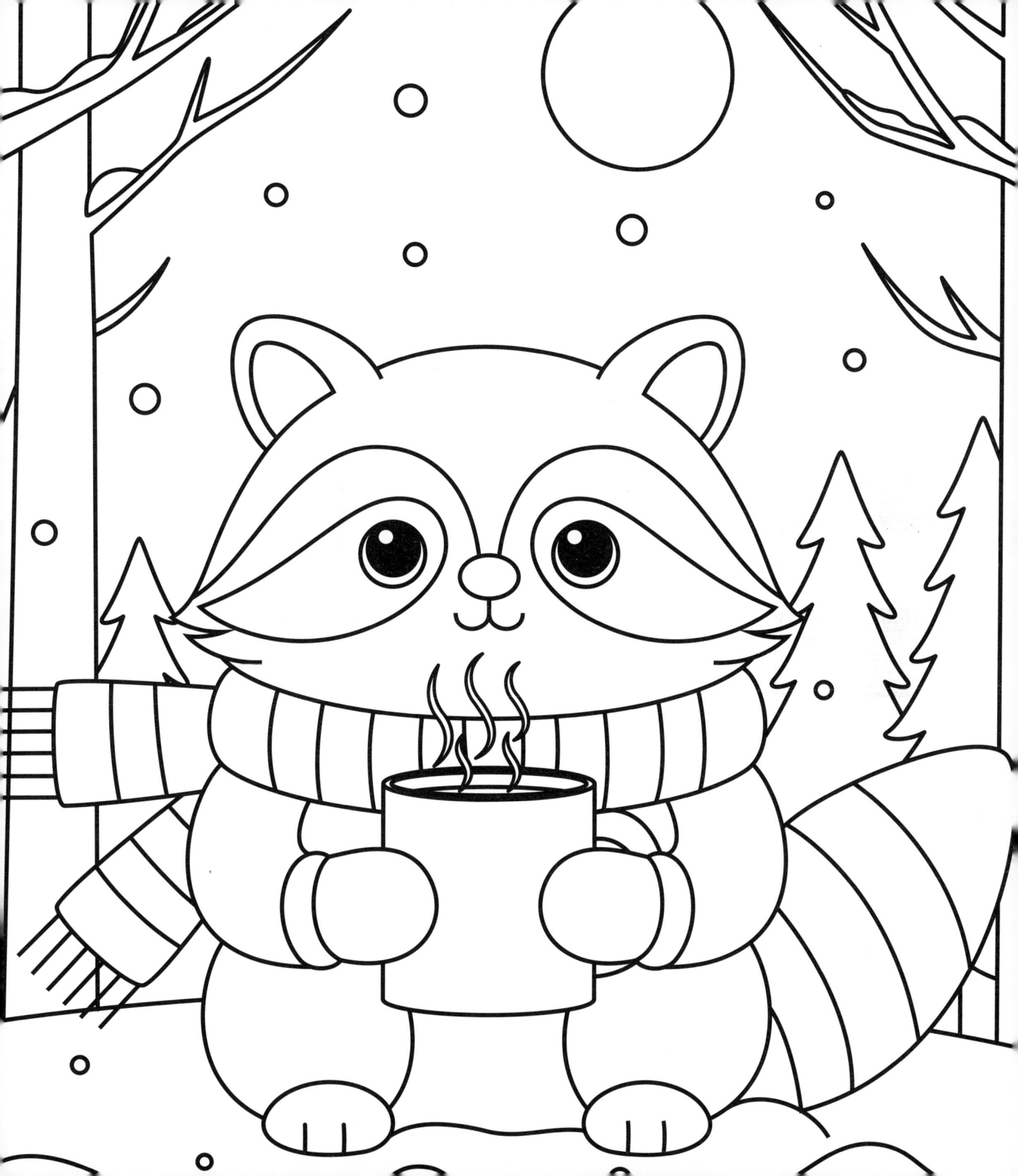

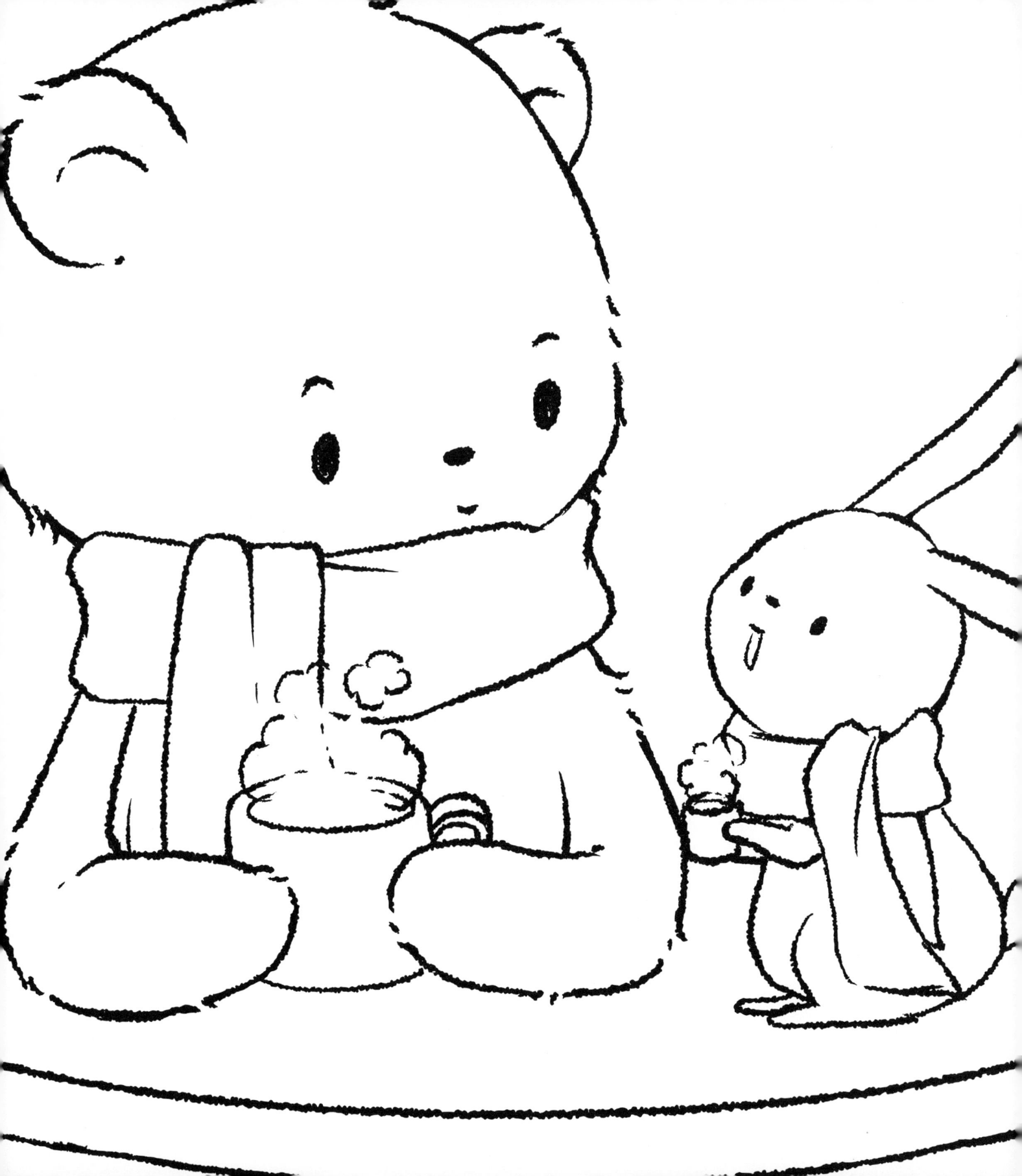

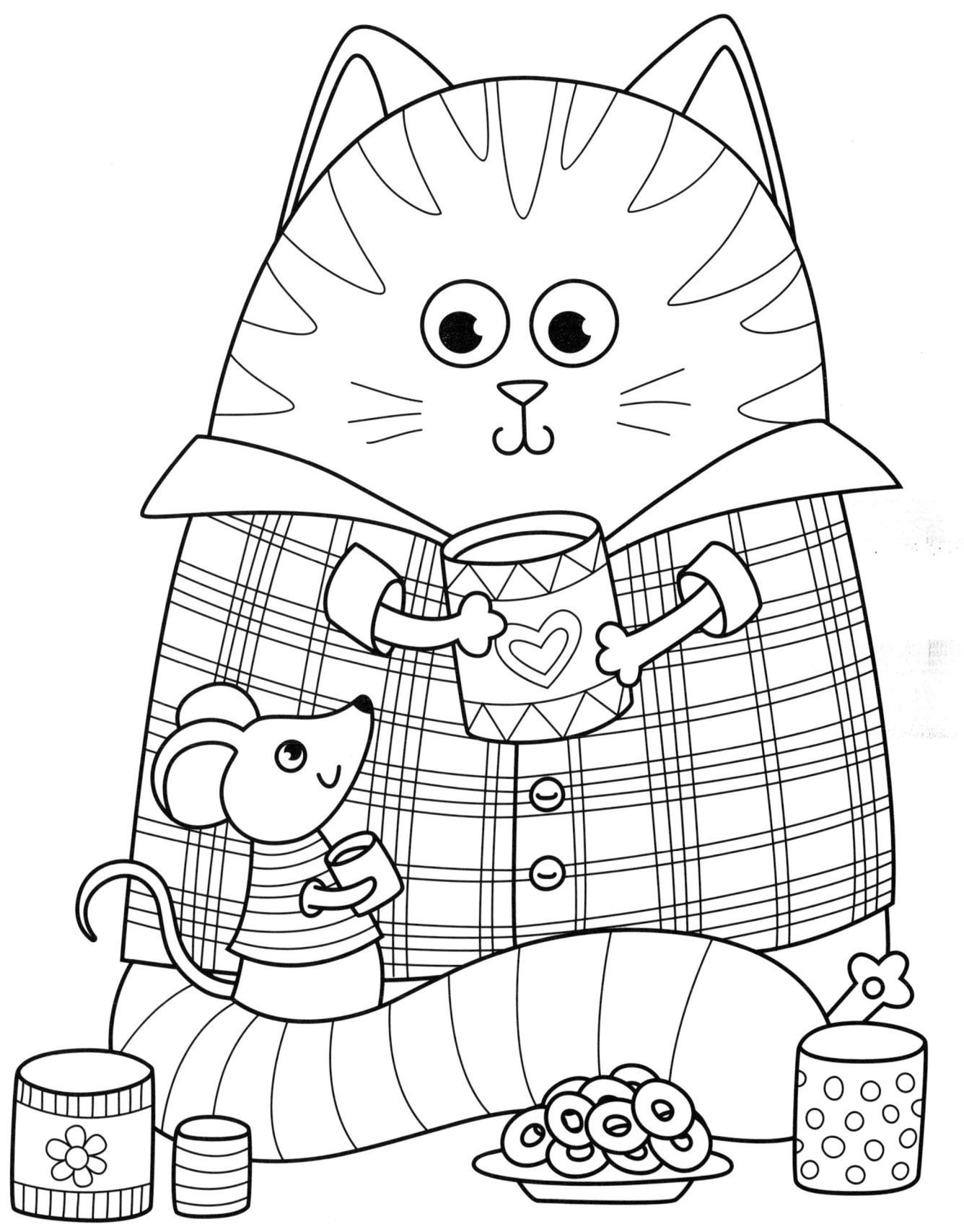

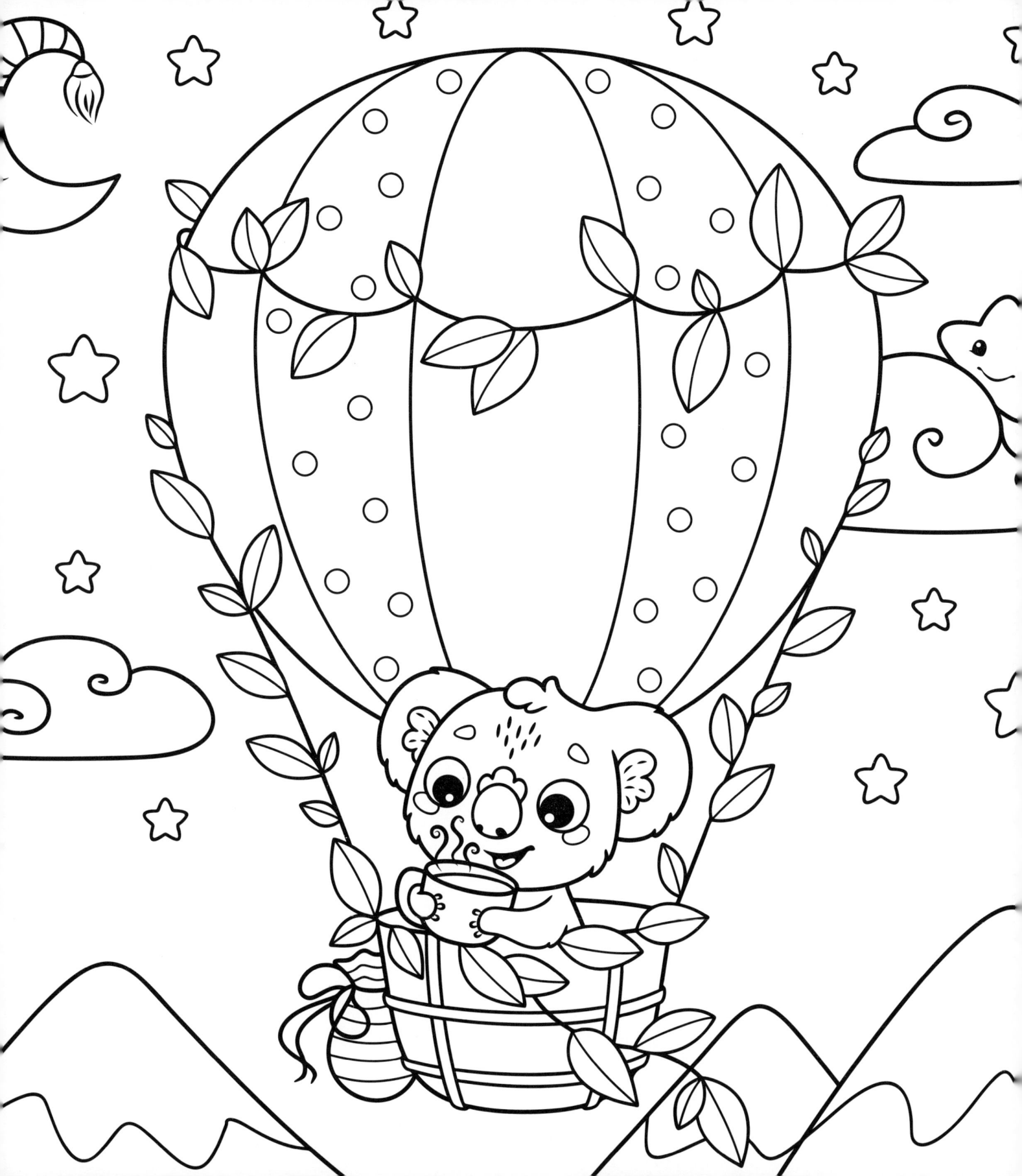

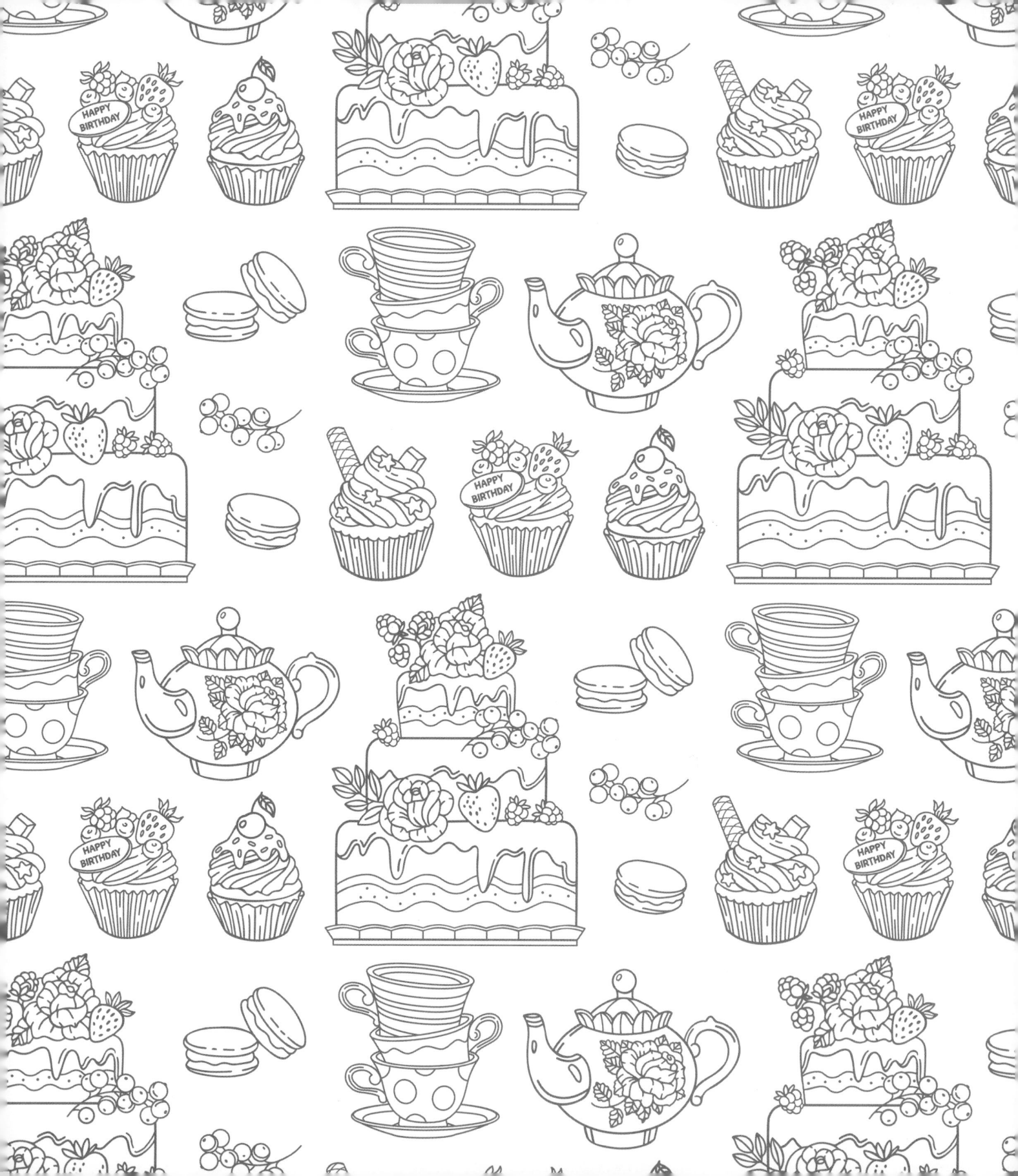

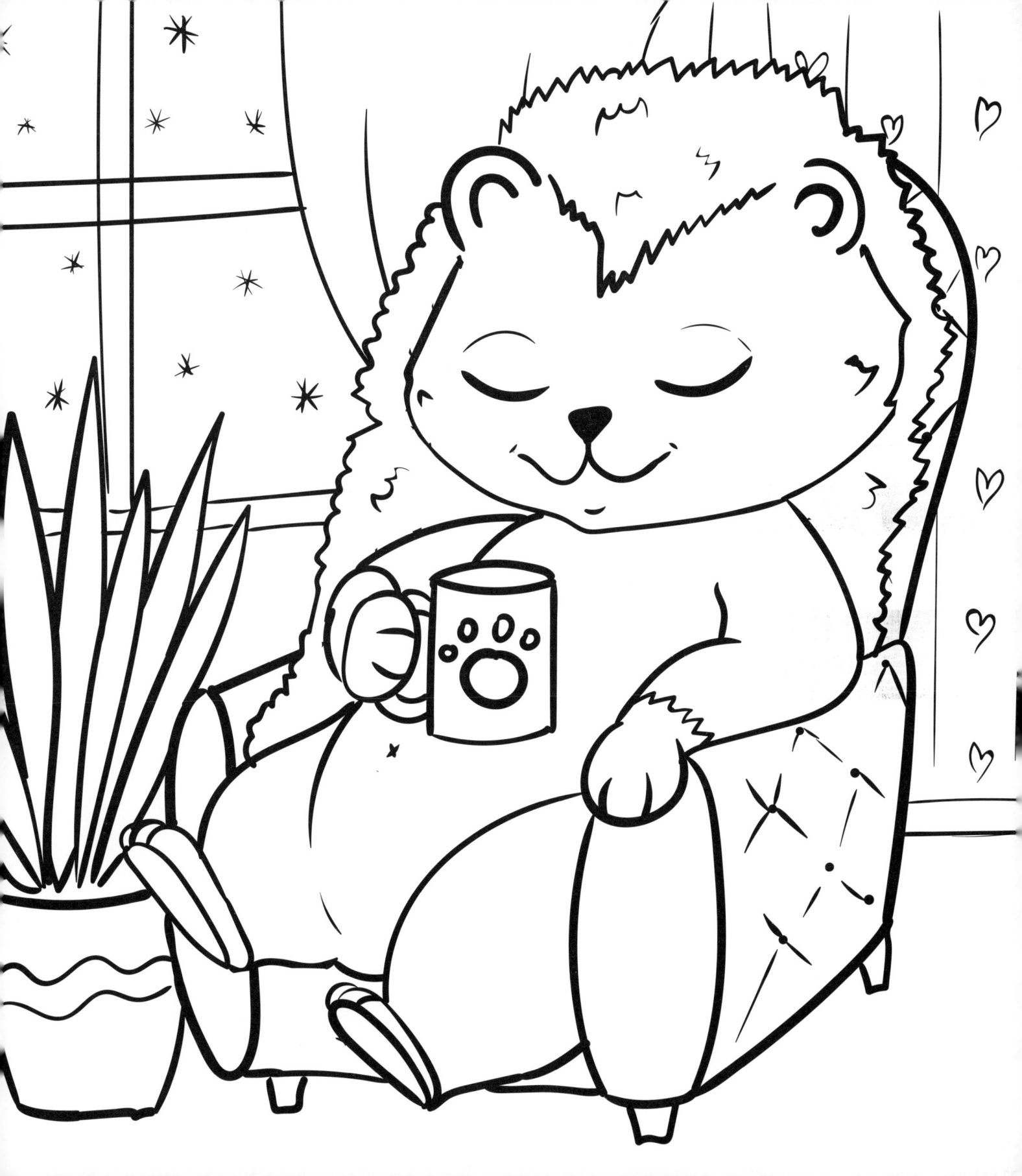

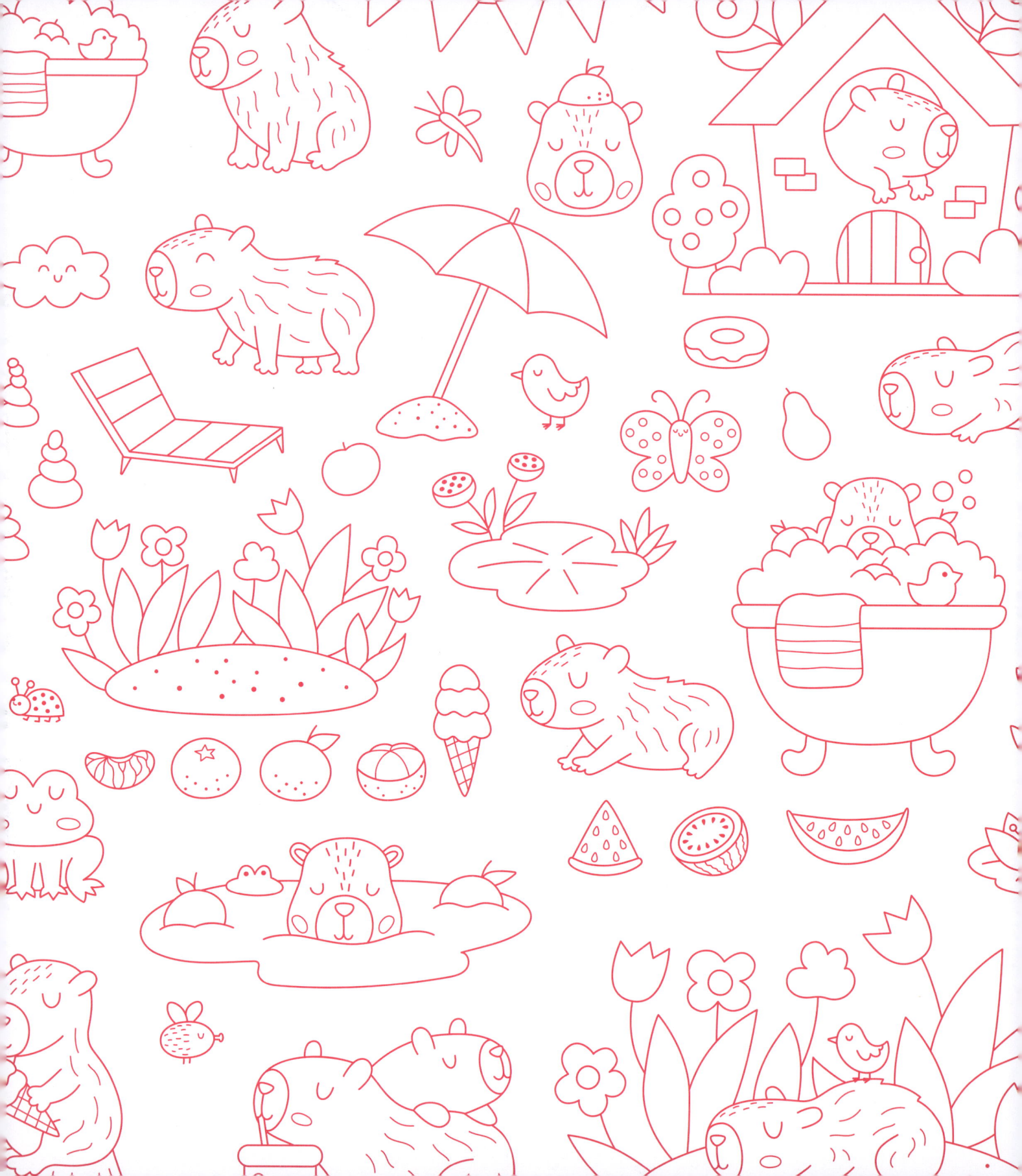

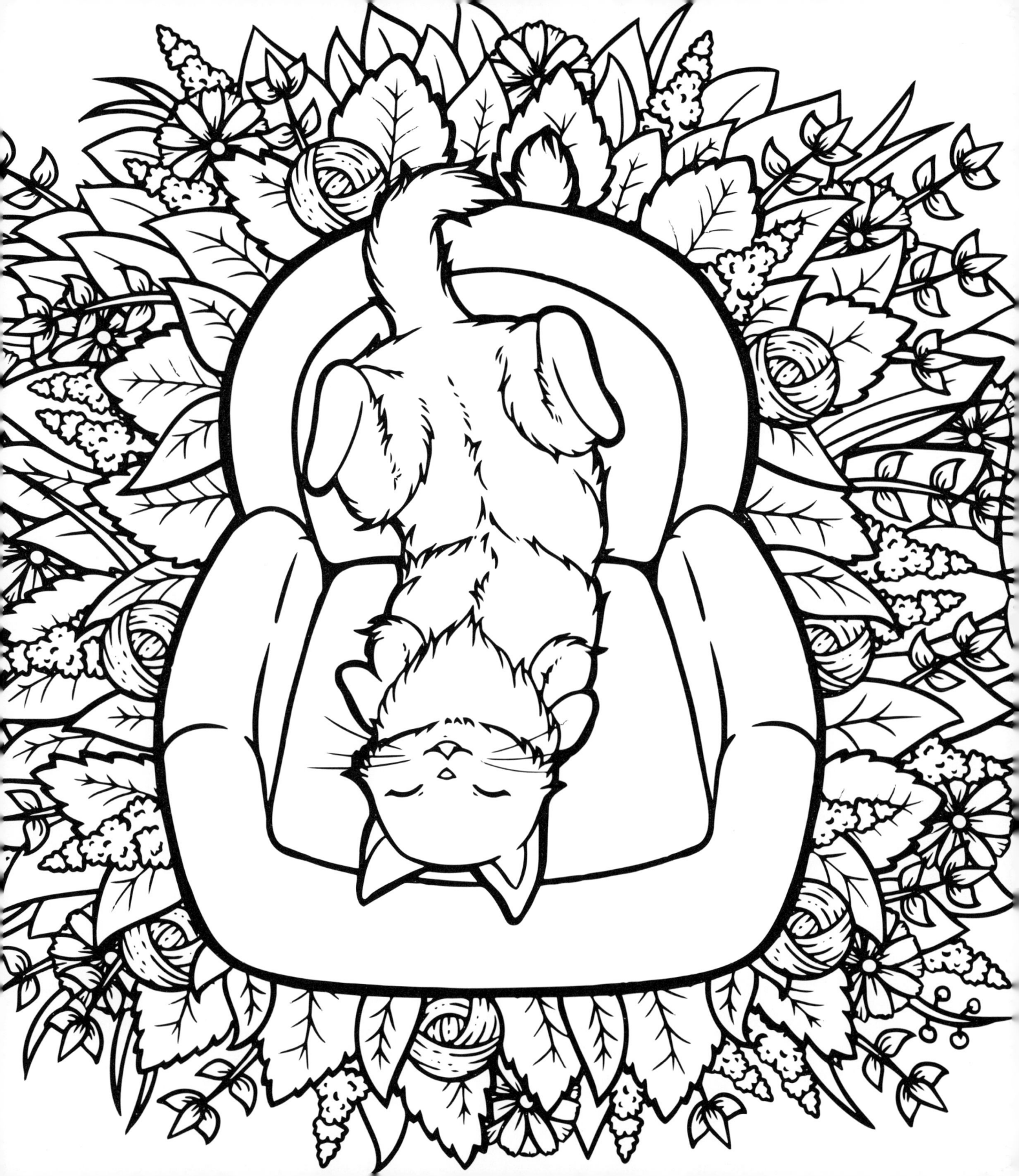

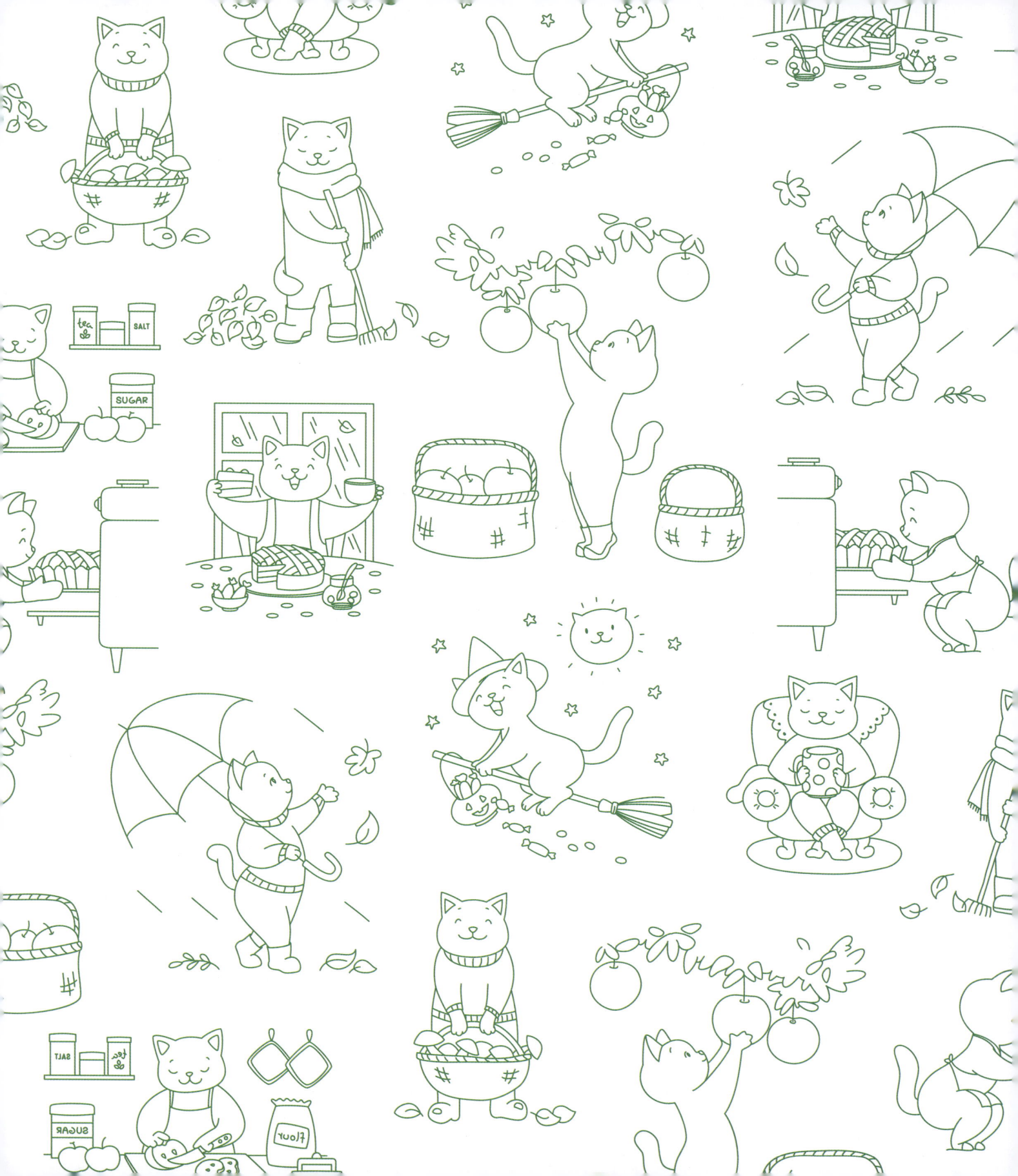

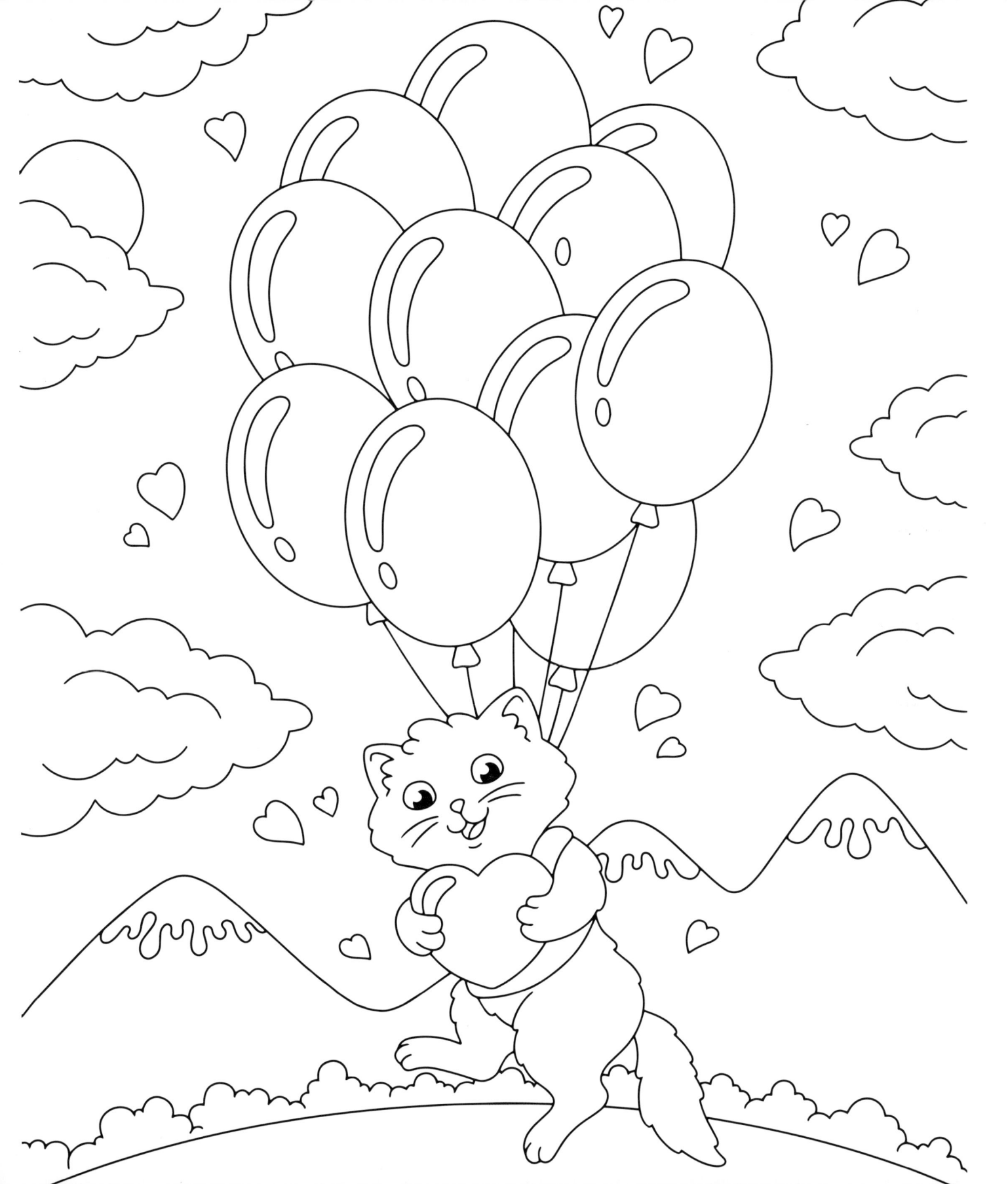

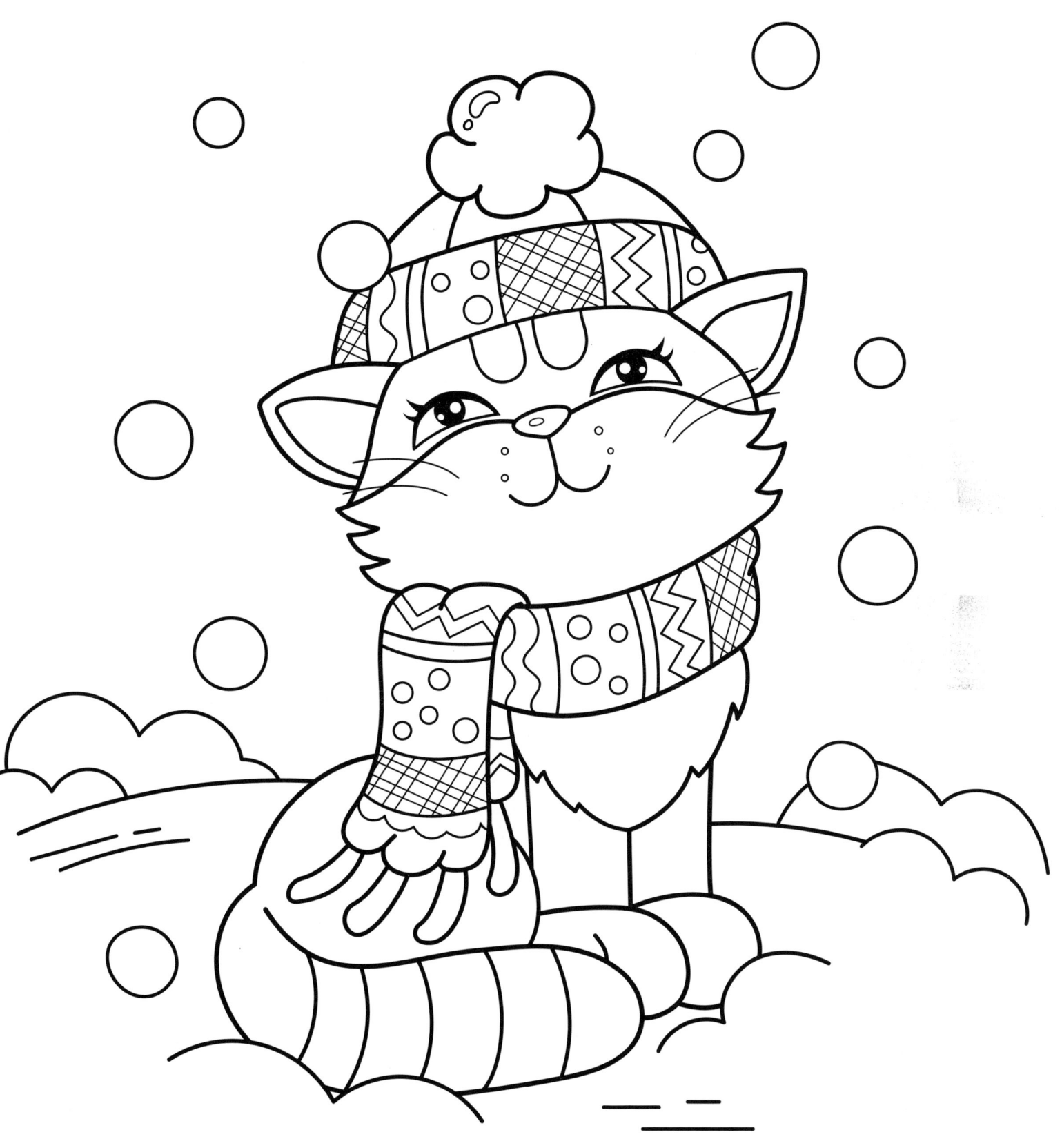

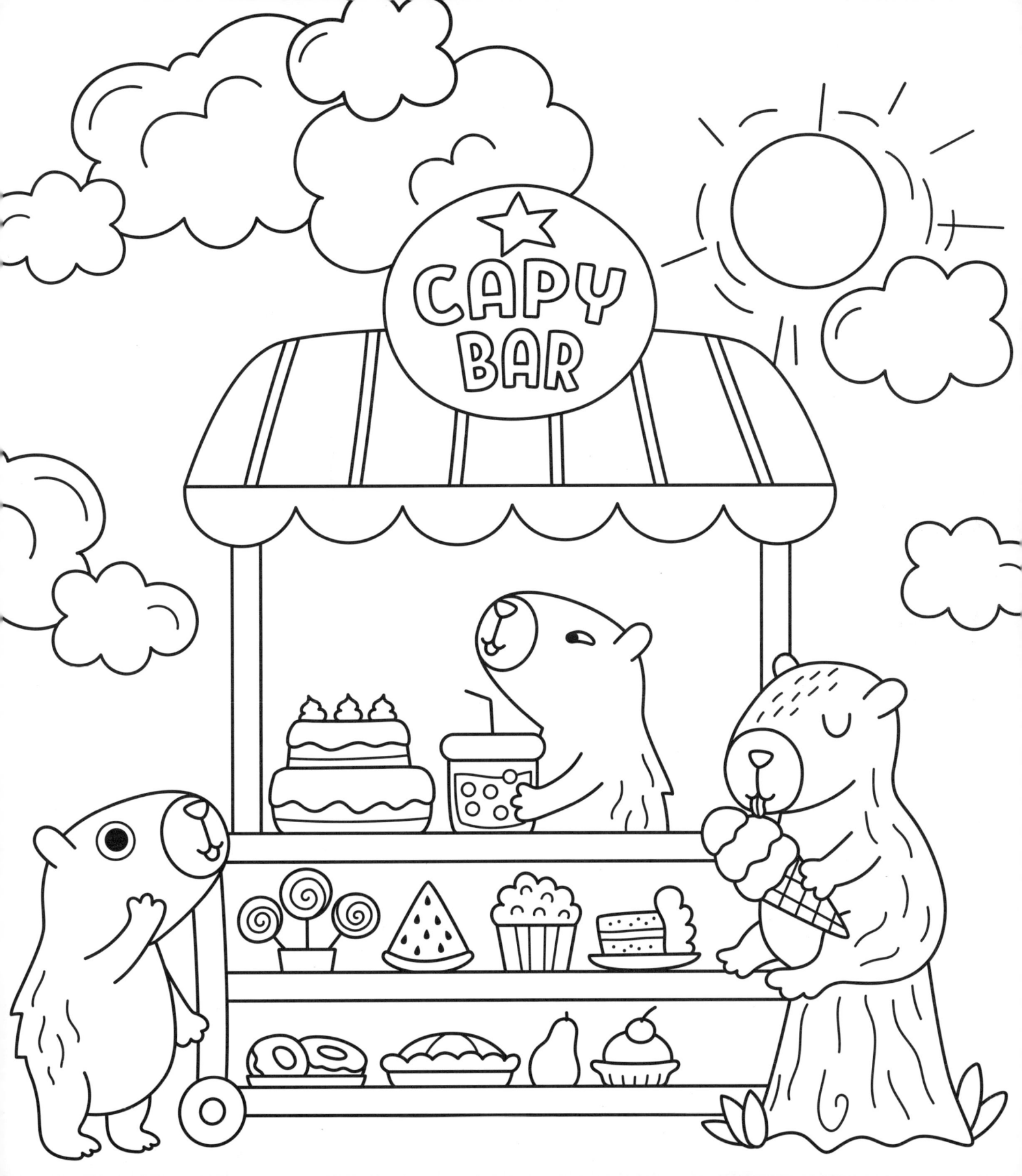

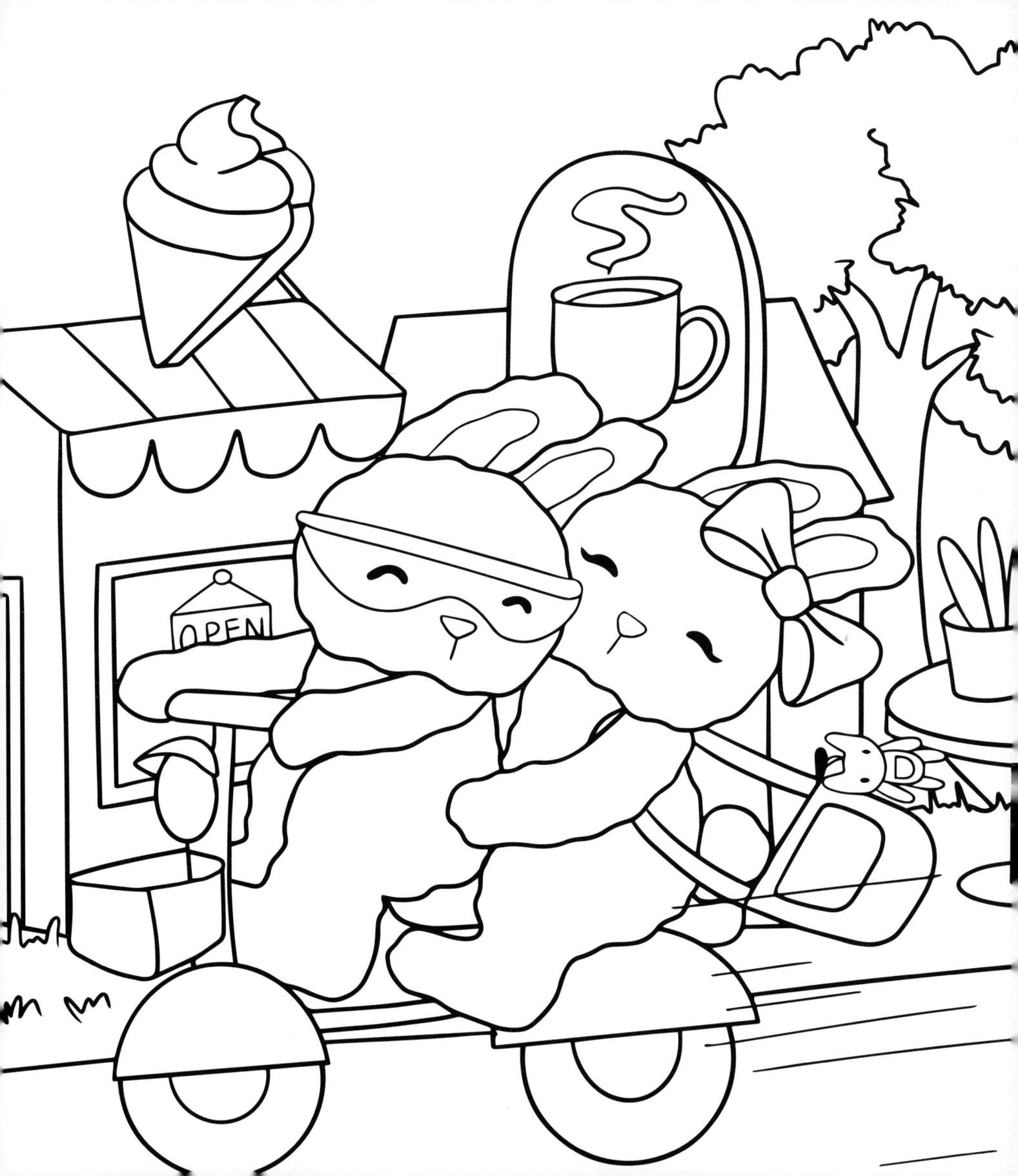

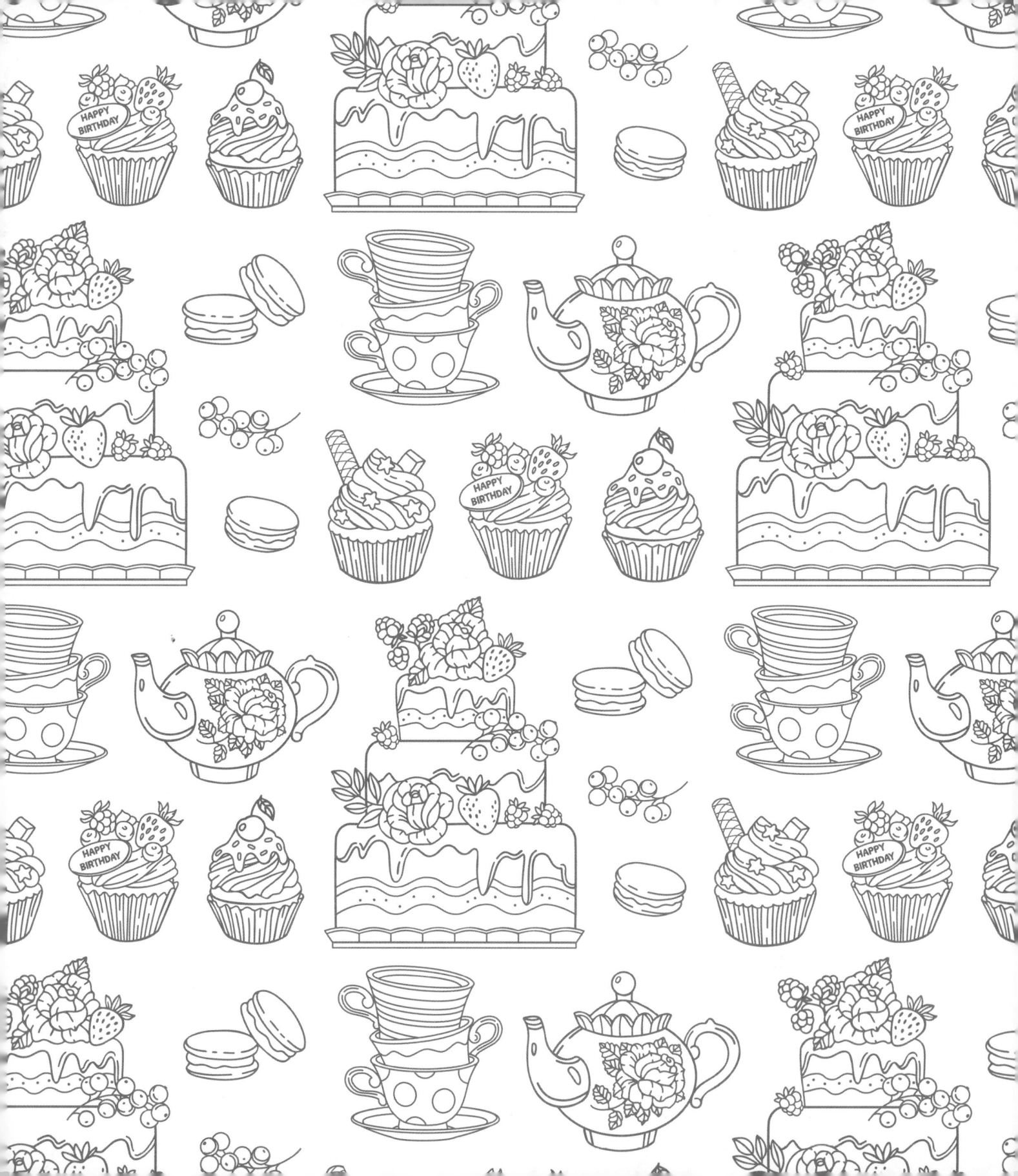

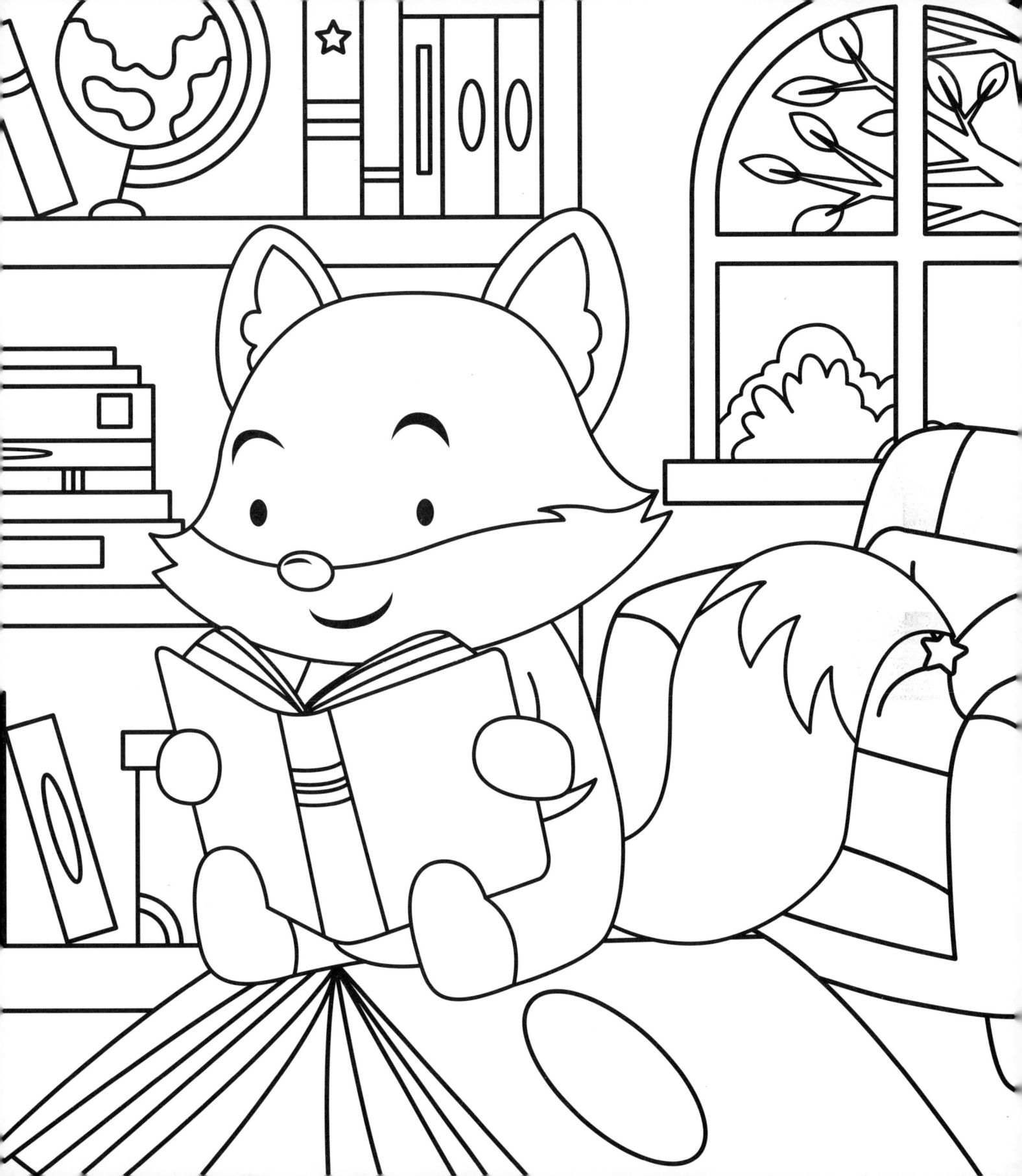

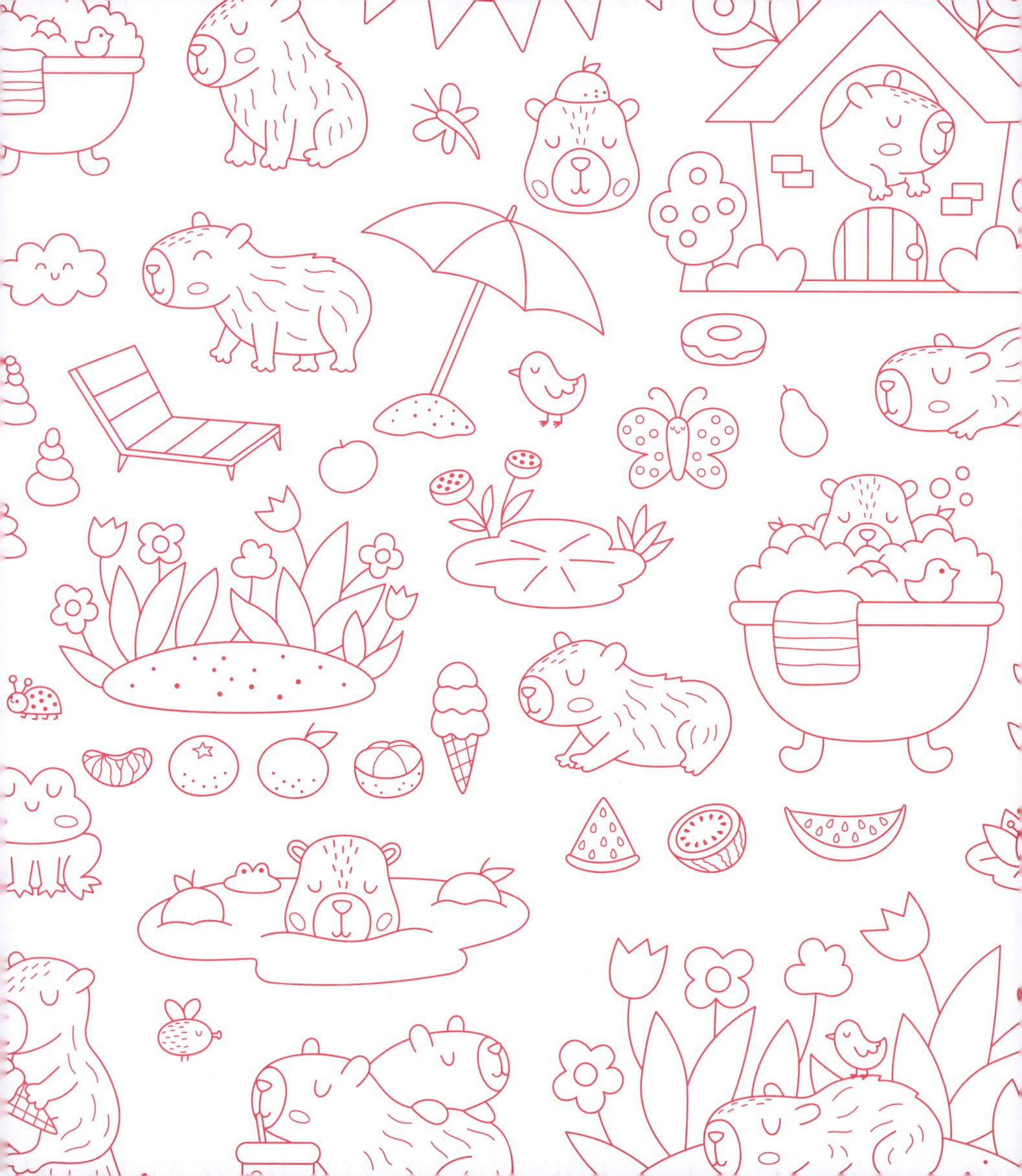

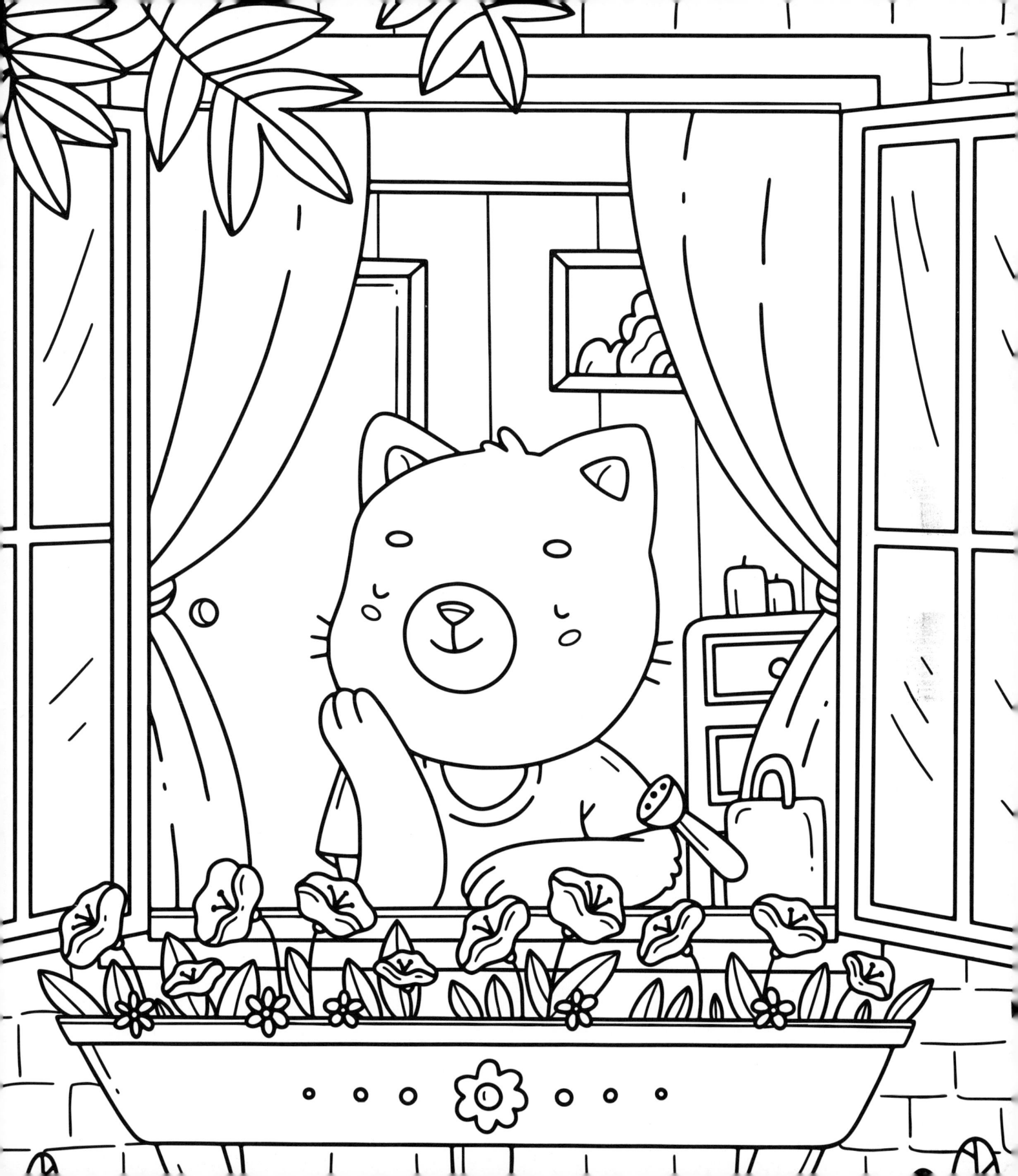

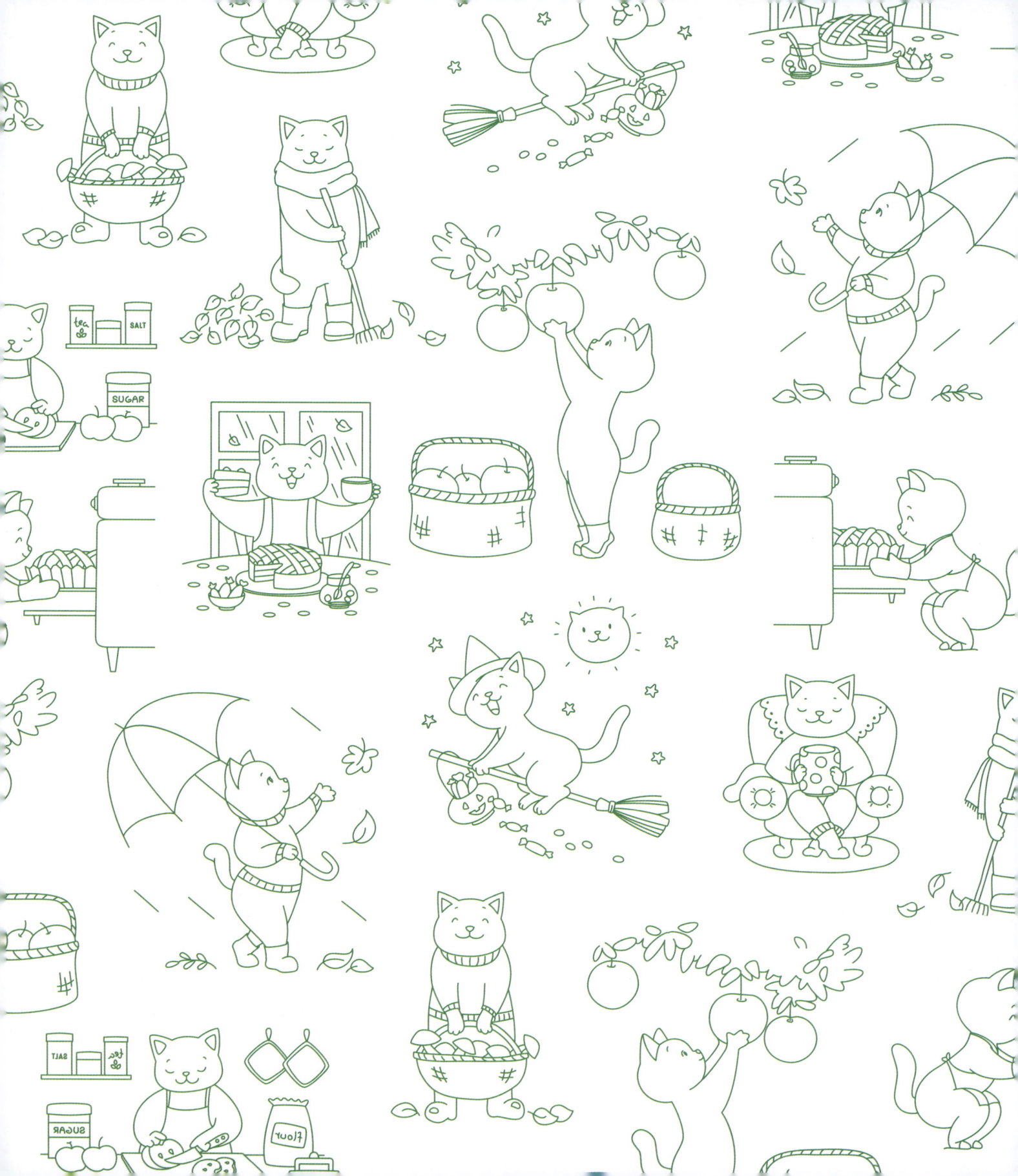

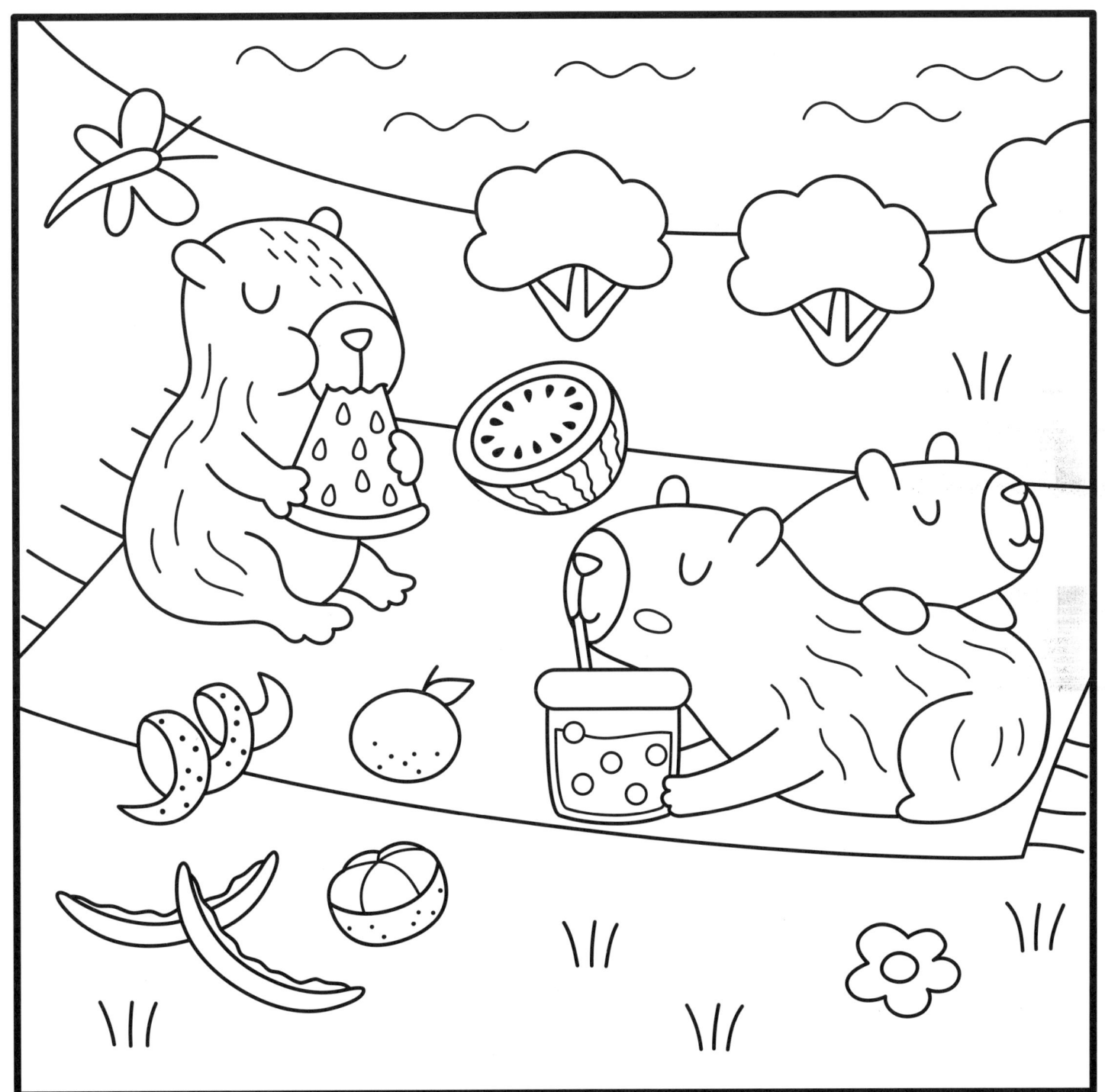

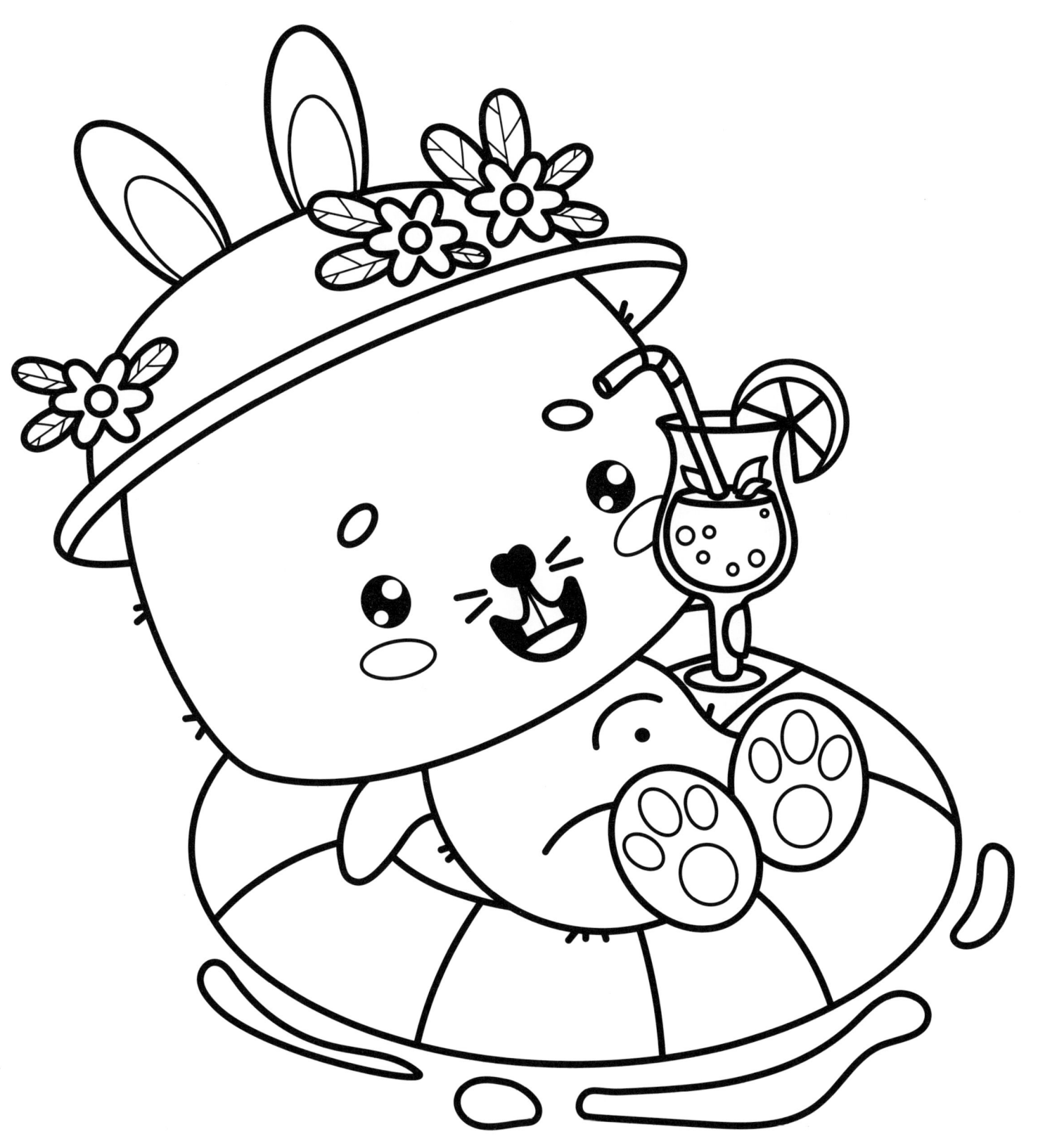

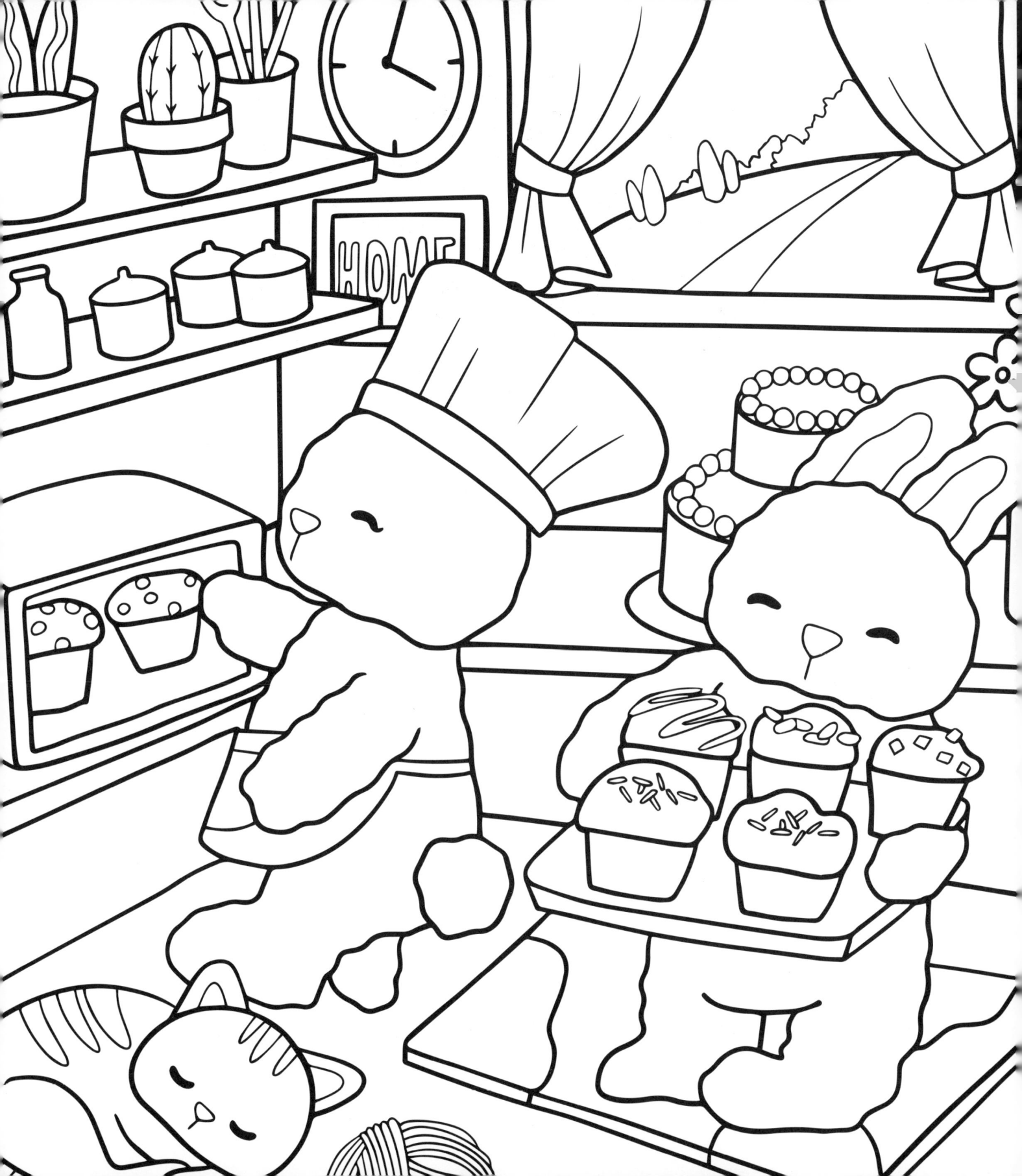

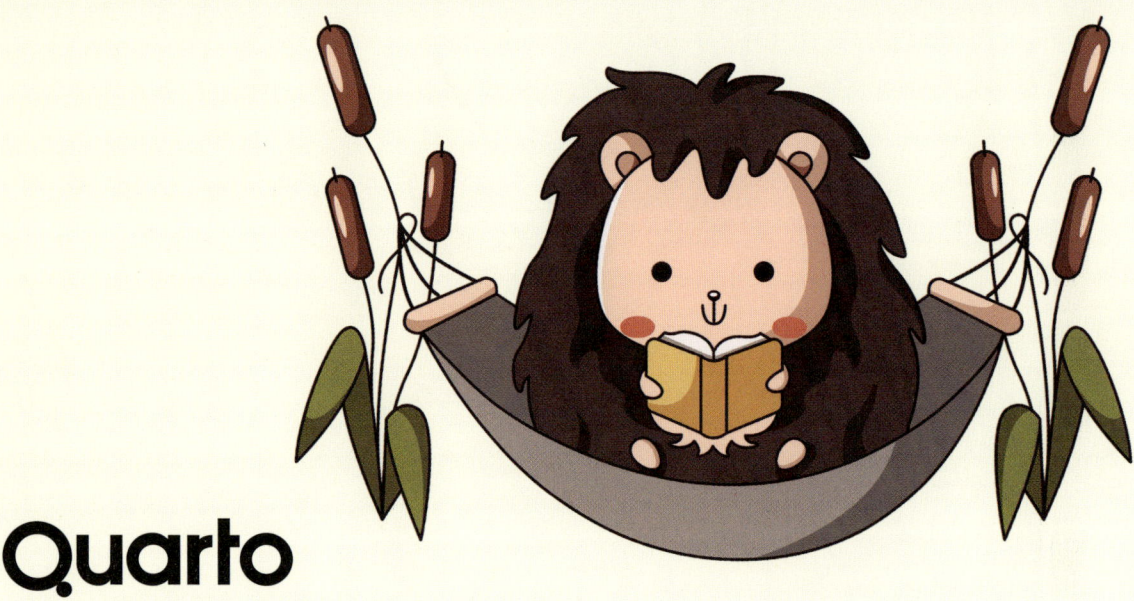

Quarto

© 2025 Quarto Publishing Group USA Inc.

This edition published in 2025 by Chartwell Books,
an imprint of The Quarto Group
142 West 36th Street, 4th Floor
New York, NY 10018 USA
T (212) 779-4972
www.Quarto.com

EEA Representation, WTS Tax d.o.o.,
Žanova ulica 3, 4000 Kranj, Slovenia.
www.wts-tax.si

All rights reserved. No part of this book may be reproduced in any form without written permission of the copyright owners. All images in this book have been reproduced with the knowledge and prior consent of the artists concerned, and no responsibility is accepted by producer, publisher, or printer for any infringement of copyright or otherwise, arising from the contents of this publication. Every effort has been made to ensure that credits accurately comply with information supplied. We apologize for any inaccuracies that may have occurred and will resolve inaccurate or missing information in a subsequent reprinting of the book.

10 9 8 7 6 5 4

Chartwell titles are also available at discount for retail, wholesale, promotional, and bulk purchase. For details, contact the Special Sales Manager by email at specialsales@quarto.com or by mail at The Quarto Group, Attn: Special Sales Manager, 100 Cummings Center Suite 265D, Beverly, MA 01915, USA.

ISBN: 978-0-7858-4727-4

Publisher: Wendy Friedman
Publishing Director: Meredith Mennitt
Editor: Caitlyn Ward
Designer: Angelika Piwowarczyk
Image credits: Shutterstock

Printed in Huizhou City, Guangdong, China TT122025